♀Life Strategy Notebook

Notebook

Mapping God's Game Plan for Your Life

Johnny Freemont III

PAGE PUBLISHING, INC.
Conneaut Lake, PA

First originally published by Page Publishing 2020

ISBN 978-1-64584-362-7 (pbk)
ISBN 978-1-64584-363-4 (digital)

Printed in the United States of America

CONTENTS

CHAPTER 1

What Is Life ♀?

For most us, life began when Momma met Daddy at the juke joint around the corner from Granny's house on North Zarzamora and Albert Street under the beautiful skyline on the west side of the Alamo City. It was under the auspices of the Motown groove to the sound of Marvin Gaye's "Ain't No Mountain High Enough" that Momma's and Daddy's eyes engaged, and their gazes locked on each other as the beat of their hearts began to quicken at the pace of a quarter horse running the Kentucky Derby. There she was, this beautiful mahogany-colored woman in a 5'2" frame with her kinky wild hair in an afro, at times pulled back in a bun, and her lovely mesmerizing doe eyes, which sat perfectly on her diamond-shaped face. As Daddy stared intently at her fresh-face, pear-shaped body frame with her small breasts, coupled with her petite waist and generous thighs, he tried to conceal the butterflies in his abdomen as he realized he was in love. Momma stared back and blinked her eyelashes and began to say within herself as the Shulamite woman said of King Solomon:

> The voice of my beloved! Behold, he cometh leaping upon the mountains, skipping upon the hills. My beloved is like a roe or a young hart: behold, he standeth behind our wall, he looketh forth at the windows, shewing himself through the lattice. My beloved spake, and said unto me, 'Rise up, my love, my fair one, and come away.

For, lo, the winter is past, the rain is over *and* gone (Song of Solomon 2:9–11 KJV).

As they moved toward each another in poetic fashion to the rhythm of the Motown sound, she looked passionately and deeply into his amorous hazel eyes. He could feel that she saw right through him and peeked through the lattice of his soul. He smiled as her luminous and radiant pulchritude called to his innermost appetite, and he finally embraced her, wrapping his skinny arms around her. He placed his small callous left hand in the small of her back as she placed her perfectly manicured right hand on his chest to feel the pulse of his heart beating, and he looked into her eyes as she pondered in her heart:

> By night on my bed I sought him whom my soul loveth: I sought him, but I found him not. I will rise now, and go about the city in the streets, and in the broad ways I will seek him whom my soul loveth: I sought him, but I found him not. The watchmen that go about the city found me: *to whom I said,* Saw ye him whom my soul loveth? *It was* but a little that I passed from them, but I found him whom my soul loveth: I held him, and would not let him go, until I had brought him into my mother's house, and into the chamber of her that conceived me. I charge you, O ye daughters of Jerusalem, by the roes, and by the hinds of the field, that ye stir not up, nor awake *my* love, till he please (Song of Solomon 3:1–5 KJV).

He then kissed her luscious sugary lips, and the journey of life began in eternity past and eternity present. At that freeze-framed moment, Mommy and Daddy apprehended one another in a love embrace. It was at that auspicious moment in time that the energy that love sparked caused you to be catapulted into a hostile environment—a race against time. You were one in a million at the nativity of life, racing against all odds to cross the finish line to get to the next level in order to live. It was you against the world, overcoming all obstacles that stood in your way. Finally, you made it! Out running and persevering against all others, you made it! And life officially begun as Momma felt a flutter in her womb, and she knew that new life had begun as you attached yourself to her uterus in the womb of worship. After three trimesters, she brought forth life through the unbearable pangs of childbirth, embracing the struggle as life manifested itself on the edge as light and darkness engaged in an eternity battle. She pushed at the cadence of the doctor's voice, sweat trickling down her forehead as her stomach muscles were contracting every few seconds, and Daddy cheered her on. He exhorted her, anticipating the moment that he would get to console her. At the final push, there you came into the world as the doctor tapped you on the backside and you took your first breath of air and cried out in the celebration of life. Daddy looked into Momma's eyes and said, "Thank you for the gift of life that we now share together in this beautiful child. I am forever in your debt!" Leaving the hospital, they made it home with you wrapped in a fresh flannel, all-cotton, baby blanket with white with blue and red strips. After entering the house and making it to the baby room, Mommy placed you in your baby bed for the very first time. Then Daddy kneeled down on one knee before his queen securely positioned at her abdomen as he embraced her and said:

> *I felt compelled to tell you and share my thoughts with you, my dove*
> *During the process of time, my reflections revealed thoughts of life and love descending from the heavens above*
> *I spent my lifetime trying to apprehend that which I have been apprehended of*
> *Which humbly bows down to the sound of the thunderous applause*
> *Of the heavenly host who witness as I reveal my heart to you, I dreamed a dream born anew*
> *To have a family and be at one with you*
> *I prepared myself for this expected hope, and nope not just*

Another dream fully measured traveling down a slippery slope
This mystical union between woman and man
Which is more profound, and cannot be measured or number
*   as the sand*
Love is about oneness, oneness with God and with the beau-
*   tiful one*
Whom my soul loveth.
To beget what has been set by the messianic banquet
Sugar, you are something special and I am not just talking
*   about the sparkle in your eyes.*
How can someone so beautiful have such a beautiful heart inside?
Most have one or the other but you have out class them all
As a full moon and the hosts of heaven on the most beautiful
*   nightfall!*

In sum, for some of us, life begins this way; however, it is much more far-reaching and deeper than what is on the surface. Life is a journey, and it has a destination. It is our God-given mission to discover our destiny, and when we do, we can unlock the mystery of life and love. Life and love both go hand in hand, and you cannot really have one without the other. Even though life began with communion between our mother and father, it was God's unchanging hand that initiated it before the world began. For it is written:

> Who *is* this that cometh up from the wilderness, leaning upon her beloved? I raised thee up under the apple tree: there thy mother brought thee forth: there she brought thee forth *that* bare thee. Set me as a seal upon thine heart, as a seal upon thine arm: for love *is* strong as death; jealousy *is* cruel as the grave: the coals thereof *are* coals of fire, *which hath a* most vehement flame. Many waters cannot quench love, neither can the floods drown it: if *a* man would give all the substance of his house for love, it would utterly be contemned (Song of Solomon 8:5–7).

The Philosophy of Life

Have you ever stopped and pondered what life is and what life is not? Initially, you must grasp the concept that life is tripartite; in other words, it is threefold. According to the *Merriam-Webster Dictionary*, life is "the quality that distinguishes a vital and functional being from a dead body or inanimate matter."[1] From this connotation, one can deduce then that life is about animation or movement. It is when matter is stirred from inertia and manipulated in such a way which causes movement by force. When something is alive, there will be growth and reproducing after its own kind. Growth is a process leading to progressive expansion. There will be struggle involved in growth because nothing can develop without it. There must be forward movement, the enlargement of the organism's orbit which is the proof of life. If you find yourself just existing and not headed anywhere (i.e., inanimate), then you are not living, and you are not growing. Anything that does not grow is dead! Therefore, we cannot talk about life without reflecting on death, which is but one thread.

A second nuance of the definition is that life is composed of a physical, mental, and spiritual reality where an individual accumulates several experiences or life events through consciousness or self-awareness. Because life is tripartite, if you are physically alive but mentally or spiritually dead, it can be reasoned that you are not fully living life to its full dimension. You can be conscious with your physical body, not invigorated, and still be alive because you are conscious and have self-actualization. You can encounter life experiences through consciousness, but you cannot act on them because you are physically incapacitated. You are extant, but to be fully alive, there has to be movement, which is driven by spirit to activate your physical extremities to allow you to be connected to your physical world. For example, a person can be paralyzed from the neck down and be fully conscious but have no moment of his or her physical extremities. This person is alive but not living life to its fullness. In other words, consciousness without animation is not living life to its full

---

[1]   *The Merriam-Webster Dictionary*, New ed., s.v. "life."

potential. Animation allows you to be fully engaged in the world and to partake of its sweet nectar, which refreshes and nourishes the sensibilities. When one does not live their life seeking all that it has to offer, it can lead to becoming functionally dysfunctional. You will begin to seek a higher life experience through drugs, alcohol, or a lasciviousness lifestyle, still feeling empty trying to fill the void. You will begin to seek anything that can numb your physical life to your mental reality because something else is missing.

Frankly put, physical life is about the following:

- growth (physically, mentally, spiritually)
- reacting to stimuli (energy outside and inside ourselves)
- reproduction (physically, emotionally, and spiritually)
- animation (movement or force)

Life is threefold. You are a spirit that has a soul which lives in a body. We are a triune being who have been begotten to live life under the sun to prepare for a transitional life afterwards (1 Thess. 5:23). Your physical life is experienced through your world consciousness. Your emotional life is experienced through your self-consciousness. Your spiritual life is experienced through your God-consciousness. If you are only experiencing one out of three or two out of three, then you are not living life to its fullness. The number three in biblical numerology is symbolic of spiritual perfection and divine manifestation. It was on the third day that dry land appeared from under the seas in the first creation account in the book of Genesis (Gen. 1:9). The fullness of time is threefold (i.e., past, present, and future). There are three proportions that make up a solid: length, breath, and thickness, which give the full dimension of an area. The *Midrash* on the number three in biblical numerology is that it is symbolic of resurrection and/or manifestation. A person must experience all three facets of life in order to receive the full manifestation of their purpose, and to answer the question, "Why am I thus?"

Let's look at all three divisions of life and what they mean. First, there is the spiritual component of life which is infinite or eternal. The spirit never dies but will live on somewhere. In the first creation account in the book of Genesis, we are told that *Adam* (mankind—both male and female) was created in the image (*tselem*) and the likeness (*demuwth*) of God (Gen. 1:26). Through the vehicle of progressive revelation, we are told by Jesus Christ that God is Spirit (John 4:24). We can surmise then that *Adam* was spirit before he became an emotional and physical being. Your spirit was created first in eternity with God. Therefore, since God is eternal, then your spirit is eternal. It is important to note that your ethnicity or the tent in which your spirit-man lives in is not the *authentic you*. The inner man is who you really are. Therefore, if your spirit is not alive, then you will continue to travel down the path of life unaware of your existential self.

Second, there is the emotional component of life which allows one to experience one of the two major human emotions—pleasure and pain. There are positive emotions of happiness and joy and negative emotions of sadness and pain. We naturally run from the emotion of pain, seeking the emotion of pleasure. We are either going to fight or run, which is called the fight-or-flight mechanism of the seat of our emotions. It is the emotional life that reminds one that he or she is alive. It allows you to experience your existential corporeality in this life. It is your passion that drives you in a positive or negative trajectory. Your emotions are the impetus which causes you to be alive and encounter life with all of its pros and cons, peaks and valleys. It is your state of mind regarding your feelings which can be very powerful, motivating, and very dangerous. According to Deon du Plessis in an article entitled "The 7 Human Emotions: The Secret to an Extraordinary Life," he lists the seven human emotions of pleasure as love, sex, hope, faith, sympathy, optimism, and loyalty. The seven human emotions of pain are fear, hatred, anger, greed, jealousy, revenge, and superstition.[2] It is important that one is aware of their emotional life and not try to suppress it because it can lead to an unhealthy mental life. The seat of your emotions exists in the *psuche*

---

2   Deon du Plessis, "The 7 Human Emotions: The Secret to an Extraordinary Life," accessed on May 7, 2019, http:// https://humanandemotions.com/the-7-human-emotions-the-secret-to-an-extraordinary

or soul. The Greek word *psuche* is where we get the English word *psyche*. One of your goals in your life strategy is to live a holistic life. Paul the apostle writes:

> And the very God of peace sanctify you ***wholly***; and *I pray God* your ***whole*** spirit and soul and body be preserved blameless unto the coming of our Lord Jesus Christ (1 Thess. 5:23 KJV, *emphasis added*).

Third, there is the physical life one lives under the sun, which is temporal. Our physical bodies are what connect us to our world. Our world conscious is based on the impulses we receive through the sensory receptors that transmit data through what we see, hear, smell, taste, and touch to our minds. Most of all, these senses are in the head. Our worldview is determined by what we experience living in this cosmos through what we see. You cannot have the fullness of life if you just experience one or two components of life. It is in the head where your eyes sit. What do you see when you look at yourself? What is your worldview? Your worldview is determined by what you believe about God, absolute reality, knowledge, ethics, and human nature. If you believe that humanity evolved from a single cell organism that grew legs crawling out of water and eventually progressed into a monkey then an ape, then your worldview regarding physical life will be different than one who believes we were created in the image and likeness of God. Moses records the divine speech of the Lord saying, "With him I speak mouth to mouth, clearly, and not in riddles, and he beholds the form of the LORD" (Num. 12:8, ESV). This scripture informs that the Lord God has a *form* (*temuwnah* [*te-moo-naw*]). Jesus was speaking to the Pharisees and stated, "And the Father who sent me has himself borne witness about me. His voice you have never heard, his ***form*** [*eidos* (*ĕ'-dos*)] you have never seen" (John 5:37, ESV). In these two scriptures, the Word of God teaches us that God has a *form*. Thus, according to the first creation account, mankind was created in the image of God.

Let Us Create Mankind

And Moses was learned in all the **wisdom of the Egyptians**, and was mighty in words and in deeds (Acts 7:22 KJV, *emphasis added*).

Moses was born in Goshen, Egypt, so that would make him an Egyptian, like being born in America makes one an American. He was an African Hebrew. Even his name, Moses, is Egyptian and means "drawn from the water" (Exodus 2:10). The culture he was brought up in was both *Kemetic* and Hebriac. Moses was educated in Egyptian ways and beliefs, what the Greeks called the *Mysteries System*. The school system was created by Imhotep during Egypt's third dynasty. His education included the belief in one God, which was promulgated by the pharaoh Akhenaton. E.A. Wallis Budge in *The Egyptian Book of the Dead* quoting two different Egyptologists states, "From the attributes of God set forth in Egyptian texts of all periods, Dr. Brugsch, de Rouge, and other eminent Egyptologists have come to the opinion that the dwellers in the Nile valley, from the earliest times, knew and worshipped one God, nameless, incomprehensible, and eternal."[3] Moses was trained as an Egyptian priest, meaning at the age of seven, he would have started this forty-year journey to complete his training in the *Mysteries*. Therefore, he was well acquainted with their cultic practices and belief systems. The Africans from *Ta-Merry* or *Kemit* (known to us by the Romans as Egypt) used the *Kemitic* word *ankh* ⚥ to mean life. It is also known as the key to life. It was this wisdom that Moses deposited into the *Torah*, which has been passed down to us today concerning life ⚥.

The *medu neter* (*Kemetic* words meaning the *Word of God*) or hieroglyphics teaches us that the word *ankh* ⚥ has two connotations: life or breath of life. According to one source, it represents both mortal life and the afterlife. So when Moses writes, "And the LORD God formed man *of* the dust of the ground, and breathed into his nostrils

---

[3] E.A. Wallis Budge, *The Egyptian Book of the Dead* (New York: Dover, 1967), pg. xci

the breath of life ♀; and man became a living soul" (Gen. 2:7, KJV), it is plausible his Egyptian education was the source. The loop at the top of the cross is a symbol that has no beginning and no ending. In African philosophical thought, it is the hidden key to creation. The loop at the top of the *ankh* ♀represents the woman's uterus, which is the womb of life, and the horizontal bars represent the fallopian tubes. The vaginal canal is the portal of life in which new life comes into the world. The crown at the top of the *ankh* ♀represents the female's energy, and the shaft represents the male's energy coming together to create physical life as we know it (see Gen. 2:24–25). You will find information about this ancient wisdom in the *Kemetic* (Egyptian) *Book of the Coming Forth by Day*, or what the Europeans called *The Egyptian Book of the Dead*.

The *ankh* ♀was used in *Kemet* and Nubia (Cush). This symbol was also used by Imhotep in the third dynasty for healing. As far as the spiritual life, *ankh* ♀exemplified water in rituals of purification. Jeremiah the prophet described *Yahweh* (the Lord) this way: "O LORD [*Yahweh*], the hope of Israel, all that forsake thee shall be ashamed, *and* they that depart from me shall be written in the earth, because they have forsaken the LORD, the fountain of living waters" (Jer. 17:13 KJV, *emphasis added*). It was thought of as the spring from which divine virtue and the essence of immortality was brought forth. In African thought, the physical body of the male and female was sacred as it was thought of as one with the emotions and the spirit. In sum, our physical lives are much more complex and interconnected than we think.

Reflection

What does life mean to you?

_____

_____

_____

_____

_____

_____

_____

_____

_____

_____

_____

_____

_____

_____

_____

_____

_____

_____

_____

_____

_____

_____

_____

_____

_____

_____

_____

_____

_____

_____

_____

CHAPTER 2

God's Design for Life

> And God said, Let us make man (*Adam*) in our image, after our likeness: and let them have dominion over the fish of the sea, and over the fowl of the air, and over the cattle, and over all the earth, and over every creeping thing that creepeth upon the earth (Gen. 1:26 KJV, emphasis added).

Have you considered that your life has a design? There is a pattern from which the Creator has arranged the details of your life for you to develop into the "authentic you," which was his plan from the beginning. He leaves it up to you to discover the gateway which leads to the transcendent life that Jesus died on the cross to give us. Your assignment, if you choose to accept, is to discover your divine purpose by discovering the pattern from which *Yahweh Elohim* works. What are you aiming for in life? Many are living with the wrong intentions and never discover what they were projected to do according to the pattern designed by God himself. Life is diverse or so vast. It is our responsibility to find out our role in the scheme of things and where we fit in order to work well with others who are on the same path of self-discovery. How do we get access to God's design for our lives? Let's explore and see…

The Hebrew Bible teaches us that God triplicated *Adam* from the beginning of creation, and mankind will remain threefold at the consummation of history when a new heaven and earth will appear (1 Thess. 5:23). Humankind was created to live in this physical world and to experience life to its fullness with our emotional life guided by our spirit-man (Gen. 2:7). Therefore, life was always meant to be manifested through progressive revelation to eventually bring one to the conclusion that the spiritual life is the transcendent life one must seek. If your inner man is the real you or the "authentic you," and if your spirit is not animate, then you are missing a very important component of life. So let me teach you…

> And thine ears shall hear a word behind thee, saying, This *is* the way, walk ye in it, when ye turn to the right hand, and when ye turn to the left (Isa. 30:21 KJV).

Isaiah, one of the prophetic voices of the eighth century BCE, was commanded by *Yahweh* to write a prophetic oracle in a book to be a witness forever against the people of God. In the pericope, vv. 18–22, in which verse 21 fits, the prophet exclaims that the Lord waits to be gracious to his people. Furthermore, in his grace, *Yahweh* will speak through the *teacher* of his people, and they shall *receive a word* concerning their *lives*. The teacher exhorts the people of God to walk in *the way* to save their lives. Jesus taught that the way of life is a narrow gateway and not many find it (Matt. 7:13–14). The path to a matchless life is strenuous; however, it ushers one into their *port of call*. Isaiah the prophet is addressing a people who had forgotten their manner of living. They were living a life beneath what God had intended. When we miss the design for our life wished for by God, we miss the mark or *sin*. As one swallows the bread of hardship and sips from the water of misery, God waits to be gracious and to exalt himself to show mercy to his people. In his graciousness, the teacher will be revealed, and your ears will hear a word behind you, saying, "The gateway to living is here now walk in it!"

God's people must make a choice at the crossroads in the valley of decisions. Laurie Beth Jones, the author of *Jesus CEO*, states, "We all are faced with two questions: Where now and what next?"[4] As one takes a minute to breathe and reflect on their current station of life, it presents an opportunity for one to review what direction they are traveling and access if you're headed in the right trajectory. The person will need to determine what the next steps are to get them to the desired place—their destiny. In other words, you must develop a life strategy to assist you with living a life well lived. One must have a profound understanding of the essence of life and its purpose to begin to develop a life strategy. One must have a plan when being challenged by a crisis. Why have life strategies? A strategy is good because nothing ever goes according to plan with some setups and setbacks. You must develop a course of action because there are unseen forces that naturally and supernaturally oppose your effort to live the life that God has designed for you. Let's see what Paul the apostle wrote to the church in Ephesus regarding this matter.

> Put on the whole armour of God that ye may be able to stand against the **_wiles_** of the devil. (Eph. 6:11 KJV, *emphasis added*)

Paul the apostle writes to the readers and hearers that when engaged in warfare, you must be covered in armor. Armor is designed to protect the one wearing it from the different weapons of the enemy. It is a covering used to shield the most important and vital parts of the body during the art of fighting one's enemy. The Greek word translated as *wiles* is *methodeia* (*me-tho-dē'-ah*). Our English word *method* comes from the same root word and is a derivative of the Greek word *methódos*, meaning "to follow after." *Methodeia* can be translated as cunning arts, trickery, schemes, or stratagems. The verb form of the word is *methodeuo* (*me-tho-doo-ō*), which can be translated as defraud, deceive, or to pervert. Why lay out the etymology of this word? The play on words is to give an understanding of why having a strategy is so important. The adversary does his work by methods to prevent you from living a fulfilled life and

---

4   Laurie Beth Jones, *The Path* (New York: Hyperion, 1996), p. xviii.

to render you powerless. One of his methods is to pervert the way of life through deception causing many to live a life of *FEAR*. This acronym is best understood as false evidence appearing real. In the *Thorndike Barnhart Intermediate Dictionary*, the first connotation of the word strategy is "the science or art of war."[5] A method is a mode of performing a particular action in warfare or conflict. It entails having a system or a plan of engagement against an opponent. Paul the apostle is writing to the body of Christ to educate us on the fact that there is a stratagem in motion against us on the playing field of life. In order to come out of the shadows of anonymity into the ebb and flow of life, you have to ask the philosophical question, "What is the meaning of life as I know it, really?" And when you answer the question, you will find you are enlisted in an unseen war against your transcendent life. So what is life?

In addition to a physical life, there is also a spiritual life. Recognizing that the physical life is not the only life is essential to being strategic in living life to its fullest. John the apostle records a traditional saying of Jesus in the Fourth Gospel: "Except a man be born of water and *of* the Spirit, he cannot enter into the kingdom of God" (John 3:5 KJV). It literally means that man has to be born from above and through baptism. It is only through believing on the name of *Yeshua* or Jesus that one's eyes are opened to an absolute reality beyond the physical world. Through the Spirit of God, we are able to see and enter into the kingdom of God, which is another absolute reality that many are not privy to. The book of Genesis helps us to draw from the well of Jesus's wisdom given to Nicodemus about the spiritual life. It can be deduced that the spiritual life takes precedents over the emotional and physical life; however, the spiritual life is the most neglected by people.

> And the LORD God formed man *of* the dust of the ground, and breathed into his nostrils the breath of **life**; and man became a **living** soul. (Gen. 2:7 KJV, emphasis added)

---

[5] *Intermediate Thorndale Barnhart Dictionary*, s.v. "strategy."

The creation narrative in the book of Genesis teaches that all life began with the Lord God (*Yahweh Elohim*). Adam's physical life was formed from the dust of the ground, which connects him to his physical world through his sensory receptors (i.e., eyes, ears, nose, mouth, and touch). However, it is the *nashamah* (*na-sha-mah*) (breath) of God that gives Adam his emotional and spiritual life. It was the Spirit or the *Wind* (*ruah*) of the Lord God (Yahweh *Elohim*) that animated *Adam*, which made him alive!

Now concerning the emotional life, the writer of the book of Genesis states that mankind is a *living* soul. The Hebrew word for soul is *nephesh* (*neh'-fesh*). According to another source, its meaning can be rendered "breath" or "inner being with its thoughts and emotions"[6]—his emotional life. The Greeks use the Greek word *psuechē* where we get the word *psychology*. Man came alive when the Lord God breathed his Spirit into him. The right spiritual life allows you to have true communion with God; otherwise, you are just existing in a physical reality and dealing with emotional problems leaving you frustrated and impotent. It will leave one with a diagnosis of what I would like to call LD—Living Dysfunction. There is no pill that can remedy this dysfunction. You have to examine your life in the physical world and come to the realization that your emotional and spiritual life are intricately connected, and you can no longer ignore your spiritual inertia. The spiritual gift that is needed to help one with this is the gift of distinguishing between spirits. Some people do not know how to discern the difference between the human spirit, an evil spirit, and the Holy Spirit (i.e., themselves, a demon, and God's Spirit). If one is dealing with a familiar spirit, it can assault on one's emotional life. In Hebraic thought, the *nephesh* (soul) is the whole person. It combines the physical, emotional, and spiritual life as one, which is different from Greek thought.

The physical life was created from the dust of the ground, but the spiritual life was birth by God's breathe—His Spirit. The eschatology of the book of Revelation teaches us that we will have a new body when the new heaven, earth, and Jerusalem come down from

---

[6] *The Complete Word Study Dictionary Old Testament*, s.v. "vp, n< nephesh.".

above at the culmination of history (Rev. 21:1–4). Paul's eschatology teaches us that we shall not all sleep when Jesus returns. At that time, we shall all be changed, taking off the corruptible *body* for the incorruptible *body* (1 Cor. 15:51–54). We can then substantiate that Adam or mankind is body, spirit, and soul (i.e., triune). So when considering a ministry to take part in, you must think about being joined to a church which promotes a holistic ministry that ministers to the whole person: relationally, spiritually, and financially. All in all, life can be described in three phases:

- physical life (*bios*)
- emotional life (*psyche*)
- spiritual life (*pneuma*)

Now concerning your *life strategy*, it is important to know your spiritual enemy has launched an all-out assault on your physical, emotional, and spiritual life. You must strategize to keep your life in order and functional. How do you develop a calculated defense against the devil? You develop a life strategy and hone your skill set of living well (wisdom)! Solomon registers in the wisdom literature of Proverbs, "**Wisdom *is*** the principal thing; *therefore* get wisdom: and with all thy getting get understanding" (Prov. 4:7 KJV, emphases added). In *Maximize the Moment*, Bishop T. D. Jakes states, "Life is a hyphen locked between two dates." He further postulates, "We need to make the most of the life God gave us today because tomorrow it may be gone."[7] In order to get the most out of your life, you must have a life strategy. Jesus teaches in the First Gospel that just living a physical life is not enough: "But he answered and said, It is written, Man shall not *live* by bread alone, but by every word that proceedeth out of the mouth of God" (Matt. 4:4 KJV, emphasis added). God's Word gives us a game plan against the modes of the enemy of our souls.

Paul the apostle teaches the church at Corinth and all churches, "But the natural man receiveth not the things of the Spirit of God: for they are foolishness unto him: neither can he know *them*, because

---

[7] T. D. Jakes, *Maximize The Moment* (New York: Berkley Books, 1999), p. 3.

they are spiritually discerned" (1 Cor. 2:14 KJV). In order to receive God's revelation or self-communication about your life, the Spirit of God must be alive in you. How do you receive God's self-disclosure? Again, Paul writes to Timothy, "All Scripture is breathed out by God and profitable for teaching, for reproof, for correction, and for training in righteousness" (2 Tim. 3:16 ESV). The apostle *par excellence* teaches young Timothy that the Word of God is God breathed. You must allow God to blow his Word into you by the power of his Holy Spirit. When you are at a dead end or a cul-de-sac on your journey and don't know where to go, let God give you a second wind and breathe his Word into you.

In Matthew's eyewitness testimony, he avers that Jesus rebuked the devil, saying, "It is written, Man shall not live by bread alone, but by every word that proceedeth out of the mouth of God" (Matt. 4:4 KJV). Natural bread will feed your physical body so that you may be physically sustained[8], but it is a healthy diet of the Word of God that feeds your spirit and emotions. In this tradition saying recorded by John the apostle, Jesus teaches, "Verily, verily, I say unto you, He that heareth my word, and believeth on him that sent me, hath everlasting life, and shall not come into condemnation; but is passed from death unto life" (John 5:24 KJV). In sum, Jesus is the living Word, and if you hear him speaking to you by the power of the Holy Spirit and believe in God, you will move from death to life. Death is not the cessation of life but separation. When a person dies, his or her spirit separates from their physical body. The breath of God leaves them and an ordained minister at the funeral gives the last rites by saying, "The undiscovered country from whose bourn no traveler returns, it has become our sad duty to commit his [or her] body to the grave: Earth to earth, ashes to ashes, dust to dust, our inspiring privilege to commend his [or her] soul to our Maker, Father, and Redeemer...."[9] The inner man, the spirit, goes on to live somewhere, either in paradise or in eternal torment. If you are at a fork in the road when deciding you want more than what you are seeing in this world, choose ⚨*life*!

---

[8]

[9]   J.R. Hobbs, *The Pastor's Manual* (Nashville: Broadman, 1962), p. 30.

Reflection

1. What is your philosophy (beliefs or convictions) of life?

    _____

    _____

    _____

    _____

2. Do you have a strategy or a game plan for your life relationally, financially, or spiritually?

    _____

    _____

3. Where do you see yourself relationally in six months, a year, two years, five years, or ten years from now?

    _____

    _____

4. Where do you see yourself financially in six months, a year, two years, five years, or ten years from now?

    _____

    _____

5. Where do you see yourself spiritually in six months, a year, two years, five years, or ten years from now?

    _____

    _____

CHAPTER 3

Wisdom
The Skill Set of Living Well

A wise *man* will hear, and will increase learning; and a man of understanding shall attain unto wise counsels (Prov. 1:5 KJV).

Wisdom Defined

What is wisdom, and why is it necessary to the strategic plan of your life? The English word *wisdom* came from the Old English word *wīsdōm* around 725 AD, meaning possessing knowledge coupled with sound judgment acquired through life experiences. Michael Heiser elaborates about wisdom, "A life well lived extends from wisdom."[10] There are two types of wisdom: divine wisdom and conventional wisdom. Conventional wisdom is the knowledge that a wise person acquires in conjunction with discernment, which is being able to distinguish or discriminate between right and wrong. A person who is endowed with wisdom exercises practicality in matters and consistently makes healthy decisions concerning the trajectory of his or her journey. Other layers to wisdom are being sensible and levelheaded. One must possess good astuteness accompanied with good ole fashion common sense to be commonsensical. A wise person must have

---

[10] Michael Heiser, *Angels* (Bellingham: Lexham, 2018), p.xiv.

calmness accompanied with sensibility to remain levelheaded in the vicissitudes of life. These three—wisdom, sensibility, and levelhead-edness—are important in acquiring the skill set of living well, which is the aim of wisdom. A wise person will hear to gather knowledge. The object of knowledge is understanding. A person who desires the skill set of living well must remain teachable and continue to learn. Finally, a person who has arrived at understanding has to grasp that a wise person seeks wise counsel at all times.

Do You Have Skills?

> And I have filled him with the spirit of God, in
> **wisdom**, and in understanding, and in knowledge,
> and in all manner of workmanship (Ex. 31:3 KJV).

A second nuance of wisdom (*chokmah* [*khok-maw*]) is skillful. It is not just enough to have the knowledge or *intel*, but knowing how to use it properly will propel you to the level of an expert. A person becomes a specialist in a certain skill set when he or she acquires the theory and applies what they have learned, coupled with navigating turbulent life events which causes him or her to continuously adapt to the changes. The skill set can be technical abilities or special skills in creating something. This kind of wisdom can be a mastery of some sort or simply the know-how to do something. This type of wisdom can be accomplished by getting a vocational skill or through academics allied with hands-on practice. Thus, to be skillful could be what you have learned to do with your hands. It can be something that you can execute with your mind because you have great vision. What skill set do you have? Have you mastered it? What do you need to do to master this skill set which will lead you to become an expert?

Are You Shrewd?

> And he said also unto his disciples, There was a
> certain rich man, which had a **steward**; and the
> same was accused unto him that he had wasted

his goods. And he called him, and said unto him, How is it that I hear this of thee? give an account of thy stewardship; for thou mayest be no longer steward. **Then the steward said within himself**, What shall I do? for my lord taketh away from me the **stewardship**: I cannot dig; to beg I am ashamed. I am resolved what to do, that, when I am put out of the **stewardship**, they may receive me into their houses. So he called every one of his lord's debtors *unto him*, and said unto the first, How much owest thou unto my lord? And he said, An hundred measures of oil. And he said unto him, Take thy bill, and sit down quickly, and write fifty. Then said he to another, And how much owest thou? And he said, An hundred measures of wheat. And he said unto him, Take thy bill, and write fourscore. **And the lord commended the unjust steward, because he had done wisely**: for the children of this world are in their generation wiser than the children of light (Luke 16:1–8 KJV, emphasis added).

A third rendering of the word *wisdom* is shrewdness. This is the ability to come to understanding of a current situation quickly and make sound judgments. It is the acumen or extreme mental focus to interject this understanding into any given situation and allow it to give you an advantage in the outcome. It allows you to see the endgame before the players get into position and execute their next move. It is being clever and displaying resourcefulness in strategic planning. Shrewdness is necessary in plotting your course on your life's journey. There will be many obstacles to avoid and overcome on the *way*. There is a saying that a truly wise person plans for setbacks and unforeseeable events in order to create a contingency plan. What is your contingency plan? What is your plan B if what you have laid out for yourself does not come to fruition? Do you have the wisdom to adapt to your ever changing ecosystem? Only the organisms that are adaptable survive and thrive to the next level. Are you shrewd enough to be aware of the next move before you have to make it?

The key to exercising wisdom when it comes to shrewdness is being a visionary. You have to see the big picture and have the foresight to see what is ahead of you. You have to be nearsighted and farsighted at the same time. Wisdom allows you to formulate processes or activities which are the sum of the vision. It is from vision that you develop goals and objectives. Objectives are the stepping stones that you follow which allows the mission to be fulfilled. Nothing should stand in your way which will cause you to abandon the objectives, and you must accomplish the objectives at all cost. Without completing the objectives, you will not be able to fulfill the mission. You must exercise shrewdness in developing the tasks and use the resources at hand to successfully finish off the objective. Purpose is the key to fulfillment of the mission (we talk about purpose later). Being shrewd allows you to take stock outside and inside, analyze the situation, establish goals, formulate strategies, set time lines, and write and communicate the plan.

In the passage of scripture above, we have a narrative about a certain rich man and his steward. An accusation was made to the rich man regarding the steward wasting his master's goods; thereby, effecting his master's profits and reputation among the business community. The rich man called the steward to give an account of his stewardship. A steward is simply a manager. Management is the allocation of scarce resources. You are a steward over the life and gifts God has given you to use for a set amount of time under the sun. At the consummation of time, you will have to give an account of what you have done with the gift of life and the God-given talents you possess. Again, stewardship is management, and management is the allotment of scarce assets. After the steward was made aware that the stewardship was going to be taken away from him, he went about settling the accounts with his master's debtors. The unfolding events of the narrative lead to the conclusion of the story, and the steward was commended for being shrewd at how he handled the crisis he found himself in. Shrewdness is an important variable in the equation of putting together your life strategy.

Divine Wisdom

Who *is* a wise man and endued with knowledge among you? let him shew out of a good conversation his works with meekness of wisdom. But if ye have bitter envying and strife in your hearts, glory not, and lie not against the truth. This wisdom descendeth not from above, but *is* earthly, sensual, devilish. For where envying and strife *is*, there *is* confusion and every evil work. But the wisdom that is from above is first pure, then peaceable, gentle, *and* easy to be intreated, full of mercy and good fruits, without partiality, and without hypocrisy. And the fruit of righteousness is sown in peace of them that make peace (James 3:13–18 KJV).

If you are going to develop your life strategy, the one thing you will need more than anything is *divine wisdom*. You must exercise the distinguishing between spirits (1 Cor. 12:10) to become aware of the type of motives operating in your life and behind the interchanges of relationships you will encounter. In the passage above, James, the half-brother of Jesus, writes between AD 40–50 to the church to educate us on the difference between false wisdom and true wisdom. True wisdom is the aim or target, but it is hard to obtain. His claim is that a wise man is one who is endowed with knowledge. He is one who produces good with a quality of modesty which true wisdom produces. It is this kind of sagacity which is needed to exude above normal expectations to reach your destination in style. The challenge is false wisdom is characteristic of one who harbors bitterness, envy, and keeps up strife. We all can be ensnared by the relationships we are a part of, and through those interactions, sometimes through intimate betrayal, we can become bitter, envious, and stir up trouble. Through our negative life experiences, we can carry burdens which are adversarial to our hopes and dreams. We can build invisible walls which can lead to toxic relationships that affect our personal and business relationships. This false wisdom can lead to self-sabotage. This kind of shrewdness is deemed devilish.

True wisdom is pure. It is not mixed with the deceitfulness of sensuality which is antithetical to virtue. Your true calling is connected to your eternal life or transcendent life. It is God's design for your well-being. We have this saying, "What God has for you is for you!" The only person who can prevent you from arriving at the destination place of your blessings is you! The quality of life that God intends for you to have must not be made lower in its quality by adding the negative energy from toxic life events and the skill set that comes with it. It takes true wisdom to overcome the setbacks and obstacles that life will politely interject on our life's journey in its attempt to fill us with bile instead of joy and peace. For example, many of us have been a faithful patron of Heartbreak Hotel, perpetually developing ungodly soul ties with individuals we knew could not love us the way we hoped. Consequently, due to these hurtful life experiences, we build strongholds around our hearts which prevent us from receiving true love when it comes knocking at our door, even the love of God. The fruit of true wisdom is a life without hypocrisy (i.e., being true to yourself with knowledge of self). Its fruit is peaceable, and we can truly focus on being what we are ordained to be before the foundation of the world.

> And the tongue *is* a fire, a world of iniquity: so is the tongue among our members, that it defileth the whole body, and setteth on fire the course of nature; and it is set on fire of hell. For every kind of beasts, and of birds, and of serpents, and of things in the sea, is tamed, and hath been tamed of mankind: But the tongue can no man tame; *it is* an unruly evil, full of deadly poison. Therewith bless we God, even the Father; and therewith curse we men, which are made after the similitude of God. Out of the same mouth proceedeth blessing and cursing. My brethren, these things ought not so to be. Doth a fountain send forth at the same place sweet *water* and bitter? Can the fig tree, my brethren, bear olive berries? either a vine, figs? so *can* no fountain both yield salt water and fresh (James 3:6–12).

In this periscope, James instructs the readers on one opportunity to avoid false wisdom, and that is how we use our tongues. In this paraenesis, James describes the tongue as fire. Like fire, there is a duality which exists with our tongues. Our words can bring health to our life, or they can be destructive based on what type of wisdom we possess. False wisdom will produce a world of wickedness, evil, or sinfulness in our lives. With our tongues, we can be judgmental, gossip, and stir up strife. We can be passionate in our speech for the good or for the bad. We can bring healing or can cause unnecessary pain. Solomon writes, "Death and life is in the power of the tongue and they that love it will eat its fruit." (Proverbs 18: 21 KJV). In its conventional wisdom, the proverb teaches that if your tongue loves death, then the person will reap the fruit of death which is separation, not the cessation of life. However, if your tongue loves vivacity, then it will reap growth and thereby a harvest. James teaches that you cannot have it both ways because something pure and fresh and something impure cannot come from the same source. Either your wisdom is from below or it is from above; you must choose the source or the pipeline to your destiny.

> My people are destroyed for lack of knowledge:
> because thou hast rejected knowledge, I will also
> reject thee, that thou shalt be no priest to me:
> seeing thou hast forgotten the law of thy God,
> I will also forget thy children (Hosea 4:6 KJV).

Solomon, the son of King David, the third king in the history of ancient Israel who ruled between 961–922 BC wrote, "Wisdom *is* the principal thing; *therefore* get wisdom: and with all thy getting get understanding" (Proverbs 4:7 KJV). An eighth-century apostolic prophet by the name of Hosea was sent by God to tell the people of God that they were being destroyed due to the lack of knowledge. The prophet used the Hebrew word *da'ath* (dah'-ath), which can be translated as "the possession of information." You will need to possess important *intel* to put together your life strategy. The most important piece of intelligence you will need is teachings from

African or Kemetic philosophical thought called the teachings of the Mysteries—Man know thyself. Jack Felder, in the foreword of *What They Never Told You in History Class Volume One*, penned, "They have a saying in Black Africa, 'If you don't know where you are going, any old road will do.'"[11] Wisdom is the skill set of living well. One must seek after it or do the necessary work to find her. An Egyptian or *Kemetic* priest who lived between 2396–2356 BC named Ptahhotep wrote in the *37 Teachings or Instructions of Ptahhotep*, "No one is born wise."[12] You must accumulate the data points or knowledge to enter into your strategic plan to set the course you will need to traverse down the path that God has laid before you to arrive at your *port of call*. Knowledge of self is an important data point which is needed, and it is intricately connected with knowledge of God.

The second nuance of the Hebrew word *dah'ath* is skill *in workmanship*. Have you identified your gifts and calling, or are you focused on your vocation? A calling and vocation is not the same thing. Wisdom is what is needed to get you on the right road that leads to the fulfillment of your destiny. You will not fulfill your destiny without knowing your calling, and you cannot know your journey's end without directions or knowledge of *the way*. You must develop the skill set of living well to be successful relationally, financially, and spiritually. According to the prophet, many do not know *the way* because they have rejected the knowledge *of the way* and have cut themselves off from their true destiny. One must seek the skill set to live well by seeking God and getting an education through vocational training or college. Vocational or educational training will assist in your calling and make the journey possible. It is recorded in the book of Proverbs, "A wise *man* will hear, and will increase learning; and a man of understanding shall attain unto wise counsels" (1:5 KJV). The two things no one can ever take away from you are your salvation and your education.

---

[11] Indus Khamit-Kush, *What They Never Told You in History Class, Vol 1* (Brooklyn: A&B, 1999), 2.

[12] Asa G. Hillard III, Larry Williams, and Nia Damali, Ed., *The Teaching of Ptahhotep: the Oldest Book in the World (Atlanta: Blackwood, 1987), 17*

> For we are his workmanship, created in Christ Jesus
> unto good works, which God hath before ordained
> that we should walk in them (Eph. 2:10 KJV).

Prophetic impartation is momentous in helping to set one on the paths of self-discovery and ultimately walking into their destiny. Paul the apostle wrote the church in Thessalonians' church, "Quench not the Spirit. Despise not prophesying" (1 Thess. 5:19–20 KJV). Knowledge of self includes knowing that you are a spirit who possesses a soul which lives in a body. The prophetic impartation will be deposited in your inner man or spirit. It is in your spirit that you have God's consciousness. It can be deduced then that divine wisdom is deposited into your spirit. If you quench the Spirit, then you are blocking the pipeline to the revelation of divine wisdom. Without knowledge of self, you will spend most of your life being led by impulses or stimuli from the world to satisfy your physical needs instead of what is needed to enrich your spiritual life. Some students change their major in college at least three times before they finally figure out their calling or what they really love to do. Some never finish their vocational training because the love of money was the impetus that caused them to enter the program, only to find out that's not what they really wanted to pursue. Therefore, wisdom is the principle thing.

A third connotation of the Hebrew word *dah'ath* (dah'-ath) is knowledge under the auspices of the spirit of prophecy. Solomon also wrote, "Where there is no prophetic vision the people cast off restraint..." (Prov. 29:18a KJV). When you think about your life, you must answer this question: "What do I see?" Are your eyes open to receive the revelation of the spirit of prophecy regarding your life? More people have given up on attending church and have sought mediums or soothsayers to attempt to get only what God can reveal. One should go to a church where a holistic ministry is evident which ministers to the whole person. When Jesus came on the scene, he went to villages and towns to teach and to preach, and then healing miracles took place. The purpose of the teaching ministry is to give knowledge. The object of knowledge is to give understanding.

Furthermore, the preaching ministry is to convince the people to make a moral or ethic decision based on their newfound understanding of their current situation. For it is written, "The testimony of Jesus is the spirit of prophecy" (Rev. 19:10b).

Wisdom through Relational Empowerment

> Two *are* better than one; because they have a good reward for their labour. For if they fall, the one will lift up his fellow: but woe to him *that is* alone when he falleth; for *the hath* not another to help him up. Again, if two lie together, then they have heat: but how can one be warm *alone*? And if one prevail against him, two shall withstand him; and a threefold cord is not quickly broken (Eccles. 4:9–12).

The next lesson in wisdom is that in order to fulfill your destiny, you must develop wholesome personal and business relationships. You must be a team player whether in a leadership role or as a follower. Knowing how to function in relationships will be key to the game plan for your life. You cannot arrive at your *port of call* without help from God and the people he will bring into your life. In the preceding passage, vv. 4–8, *Qoheleth* described the vanity of living life just working to make money in pursuit of materialistic things. He describes his observation of this kind of life under the sun. He recorded that there will be envy from one's neighbor when you toil and use your skills to carve out a life in this world. As he discerned this, he came to this conclusion that all is *hebel* (*heh'vel*) or vanity, which is fruitlessness. The selfish toil that we sometimes chase after is absurd as trying to lay hold of the wind. The best course of action is to partner with someone who has similar goals and aspirations. The eighth-century prophet Amos penned, "Can two walk together except they be agreed" (Amos 3:3 KJV)? In other words, there has to be a meeting of the mind-sets in the pursuit of wisdom. The fool folds his or her hands (i.e., an attitude of lethargy) which are antithetical to a wise person.

In v. 9, *Qoheleth* or the *Preacher* gives the command that two are better than one. The best reward is the labor of partnership with one who is traversing down the same path as you. He lists the benefits of a healthy relationship with one who shares your destiny. Failure is inevitable, and failure is the professor of life. When you fall, it is a benefit to have a partner to help lift you up. Solomon wrote in the fall season of his life, "A just man falleth seven times and riseth again" (Prov. 24:16a). When the temperature of living goes down below freezing, it will behoove you to have someone to help you keep warm. In this life under the sun, you will encounter many adversaries; it is strategic to have someone who can watch your back. Finally, *Qoheleth* gives the most profound wisdom on healthy relationships with the reference to a threefold cord which is not easily broken. Again, the number three in biblical numerology is representative of spiritual perfection. A relationship with God the Father and Jesus Christ through the fellowship of the Holy Spirit is what strengthens all relationships.

Wisdom through Financial Empowerment

> He that is faithful in that which is least is faithful also in much: and he that is unjust in the least is unjust also in much. 11 If therefore ye have not been faithful in the unrighteous mammon, who will commit to your trust the true *riches*? (Luke 16:10–11 KJV).

Financial empowerment is crucial to your life's strategic plan. Some of us grew up in family systems that did not live by a budget but paycheck to paycheck. The first nugget of wisdom is never pay out more than you bring in. You will forever live your life in arrears paying past due bills to avoid an interruption in your utilities or services. *Qoheleth* states, "Money answereth all things" (Eccles. 10:19 KJV). Therefore, money is important, and how we handle it is crucial to having life and having it more abundantly. In the scripture above, Luke teaches a lesson about true faithfulness. If a man or woman is faithful in a little thing, then he or she will be faithful in much. On the contrary, if he or she is unjust in little, then they will be unjust in much. If you can adhere to a budget when you have little, then you will be responsible in handling money when your income increases. On the other hand, if you spend more than you make when you have a little money, the more money you make, the more you will spend, leaving you in the same condition. If you want God to bless your efforts, then you have to be faithful over a little. Solomon writes, "The blessing of the LORD, it maketh rich, and he addeth no sorrow with it" (Prov. 10:22 KJV). This is wisdom. The materialistic things are not the blessings of the Lord. Rather, God's favor is the blessing.

Wisdom through Spiritual Empowerment

> The fear of the LORD *is* the beginning of wisdom: and the knowledge of the holy *is* understanding (Prov. 9:10 KJV).

It is the Spirit that gives life. Wisdom is acquired by having a reverence for *Yahweh Elohim* (the Lord God) because he is the gateway to the divine revelation and prophetic impartation in one's life. It is through worshipful submission to one who is above you which starts you on the journey to self-actualization. It is through special revelation that God's self-communication instructs one in the way of life. The proper response is reverent obedience, which is the key that gives one access to wisdom. It all begins with respect of the *Divine Dispenser* or *Giver* of wisdom. Piety, truth, and wholesomeness are the linchpins which keep you on path to your destiny.

Reflection

On this page, list your *likes*, dislikes, *work values*, and the *geographical location* where you would love to work and live. Write a purpose statement for your life.

Interest, Likes, Dislikes, and Hobbies

Write down your likes: _____

_____

Write down your dislikes: _____

_____

What are your interests: _____

_____

Write down your hobbies: _____
Have you thought about completing your vocational training?

_____

Have you thought about going back to finish your college degree?

_____

Write down what do you love to do even if you did not get paid to do:

_____

_____

_____

_____

_____

_____

_____

_____

_____

CHAPTER 4

A Life ⚲of Purpose
A Purpose Driven Life
vs. Unfilled Life

Counsel (*purpose*) in the heart of man *is like* deep water; but a man of understanding will draw it out (Prov. 20:5 KJV, *emphasis added*)

Is your existence a life of aspiration or ambition to achieve your purpose? If so, what is your motivation? Can you sketch your purpose if asked to share it? Purpose has to do with personal meaning and having a sense of direction as you are traversing down the path that God has set before you. It is living your life knowing that it is a life not by accident. It is coded in your subconscious as a goal that speaks to you in a "still small voice," pushing you toward an end result. Socrates taught his pupil Plato that "the unexamined life is not worth living." A purpose driven life is one in which the person is constantly taking inventory of their existence to investigate and evaluate if they are where they should be. They learn the rules of the game of life and ensure they know the objectives because they play to win. No one participating in a game plays without knowing the objectives and the rules because that leads to defeat or failure. Jones states, "Discovering your purpose causes us to reexamine 'who we are' and 'what we are really about.'"[13] In chapter 3 of his book entitled *In Pursuit of Purpose*,[14] Dr. Myles Munroe outlines the principles of purpose:

- The Lord God is a Creator of purpose.
- All of creation has an aim, which is God's intent.
- Not every cause has been unveiled or revealed.
- When the goal of a thing is not recognized and acknowledged, misdirection takes place.
- If you want to know the cause of something, look to its design and its designer.
- The intelligent design of a thing can only be discovered from its Maker—the Great Architect of the cosmos.
- Knowing one's intent for being is the key to accomplishment and/or actualization. Because your being flows out of your doing.

Myles Munroe's seven principles of purpose seem to answer the much-anticipated question, "How do I find true happiness?" You can make yourself blissful or content by discovering your purpose. Fulfillment is the means to happiness. In the praise of happiness or blessedness, David in Psalm 1 gives some important wisdom to understanding what it means to be happy—live by questing after purpose.

> Blessed (*or happy*) *is* the man that walketh not in the counsel of the ungodly, nor standeth in the way of sinners, nor sitteth in the seat of the scornful. But his delight *is* in the law of the LORD; and in his law doth he meditate day and night. And he shall be like a tree planted by the rivers of water, that bringeth forth his fruit in his season; his leaf also shall not wither; and whatsoever he doeth shall prosper. (Ps. 1:1–3 KJV, *emphasis added*)

[13] Jones, *The Path*, p. ix.
[14] Myles Munroe, *In Pursuit of Purpose* (Shippensburg: Destiny Image, 1992), pp. 27–40.

> ➤ To be happy or blessed, you must *avoid* taking advice from people who do not walk with God or who are not saved. These are people who have not accepted Jesus Christ as their Lord and Savior or wolves in sheep's clothing (WISC's)! These people are devoid of purpose. The prophet asked the proverbial question, "Can two walk together, except they be agreed" (Amos 3:3 KJV)?

> ➤ To be happy or blessed, you *must not* find yourself standing or at standstill in the same way of life as sinners—those who continue to live life without purpose and who miss what God's plan is for their life!

> ➤ To be happy or blessed, you must *avoid* being situated with those who mock living a godly life, constantly seeking after God!

If you follow these proscriptions, you will be like a tree that bends but does not break amid storms and under the pressures of life. By making God the center of your orbit—your personal cosmos— you will produce fruit (tangible results) in your season (or at the *appointed* time)! In order to produce fruit, you must plant seeds (the Word, God's wisdom) and have a good water supply (the Holy Spirit, God's power). You must irrigate the field of your dreams. You must invest (*sow*) into your vision and cross-pollinate with the right people to catapult you into your destiny. Having a destiny implies that you must have a destination! You must ask the rhetorical question, "Where am I headed?" Jesus of Nazareth must become your road map who will assist you in getting to your divine destination. All in all, keep praying (talking) to God, praising him for what you do not see in the natural but discern in the spirit. Following these steps will establish the prophetic word spoken over your life, and it will come to pass at the appointed time.

> **Trust** in the LORD, and **do good**; *so* shalt thou dwell in the land, and verily thou shalt be fed. **Delight** thyself also in the LORD; and he shall give thee the desires of thine heart. **Commit** thy way

unto the LORD; **trust** also in him; and **he shall bring *it* to pass.** (Ps. 37:3–5 KJV, *emphasis added*)

King David expresses poetically in this psalm to fret not! In the Hebraic expression, this fretting or the burning with anger or worry is brought upon oneself. David is telling the readers and hearers of God's Word from personal experience not to be anxious about those who do not follow God and are not led by his Spirit. Trust in whom then? The alternative is to trust in God and not eat your heart out over "what's next." He offers a solution to have confidence in the Lord, and he will give you the aspiration and bring your purpose to pass. To live in your purpose, you must do the following:

➢ trust (in the Lord)
➢ do good (watch what you do and who with)
➢ dwell (have staying power until God says move)
➢ delight (praise God for what he is doing right now where he has you)
➢ commit (persevere and work the game plan until it is finished)

Solomon wrote, "The **purpose** in a man's heart is like deep water, but a man of **understanding** will draw it out" (Prov. 20:5 ESV, *emphasis added*). He uses the Hebrew word `etsah (ay-tsaw')` which can be translated as "to give counsel, design, or purpose." It can be deduced that your purpose must be drawn out from the deep reposits of your inner man (your heart). There is a blueprint of your life sketched by an Intelligent Designer, but you must go beyond the physical, rise above the emotional, and tap into the spiritual to draw it out through progressive illumination with signs of revelation.[15]

The heart of a man in Hebraic thought is the inner person who can discern spiritual things. It is that part of us where the rational

---

[15] Donald K. McKim, *Westminster Dictionary of Theological Terms* (Louisville: Westminster John Knox, 1996), p. 240. Signs of revelation are" …God's revelation as an event in which humans encounter God."

thinking process takes place. One expositor stated, "The heart is the fountain of a man's deeds."[16] A man's or woman's purpose spring from the source, which is positioned in his or her heart. The Hebrew word for heart is *lēb* (pronounced *labe*). In the *BDB Hebrew and English Lexicon*, the word can be rendered[17]:

- the seat of desire, inclination, or will
- an aspect of personality
- the mind, conscience, the seat of your appetites, and emotions

Since Moses is the author of the book of Genesis, let's investigate where he would have gained this understanding of the heart. Luke, the physician, chronicles for us in Stephen's speech before the Jewish leaders, "And Moses **was learned in all the wisdom of the Egyptians**, and was mighty in words and in deeds" (Acts 7:22 KJV, *emphasis added*). In the African book *The Coming Forth by Night and Day* (Europeans called it *The Egyptian Book of the Dead*), it teaches that the heart is considered "the seat of the power of life," as well as the pipeline of a good or bad thought life.[18] If the origin of purpose is found in the heart, when we discover purpose, we tap into a limitless power source. In African wisdom literature such as *The Teachings of Ptahhotep* (edited by Asa Hilliard III, Larry Williams, and Nia Damali), Ptahhotep teaches, "Follow your heart as long as you live. Do no more than is required. Do not shorten the time of 'follow the heart,' since that offends the Ka."[19] Your heart must be pure to follow the wisdom of Ptahhotep and to gain access to the power of God from within. It must be washed in the water of the Word, consecrated or set apart for God's purposes, and sanctified in the blood of the Lamb of God. After all, Jesus did say, "Blessed *are* **the pure**

---

[16] *Vine's Complete Expository Dictionary of Old and New Testament Words*, r.v. "heart."

[17] BDB, r.v., "ble""

[18] E.A. Wallis Budge, *The Egyptian Book of the Dead* (New York: Dover, 1967), p. lxi.

[19] Asa G. Hilliard III, Larry Williams, and Nia Damali, ed., *The Teachings of Ptahhotep: The Oldest Book in the World* (Atlanta: Blackwood, 1987), p. 21.

in heart: for they shall see God" (Matt. 5:8 KJV, *emphasis added*). Therefore, you will have to get your bucket out with enough rope to go deep into your *áb* (the Egyptian/Kemetic word for *heart*) to draw out the intelligent design for your life.

The unfulfilled life is living or existing without purpose, aimlessly shooting without regard for the target. It is the perpetual meandering through life without passion or focus. It is a barrage of systematic failures and countless setbacks, forever missing the mark that God has set for you—sin. Instead of discovering happiness or blessedness, the person's life is a life that is bitter, frustrated, and an existence without relevance or significance. This type of person finds themselves in toxic relationship after toxic relationship. They are always in financial trouble, living from paycheck to paycheck. They lack the spiritual empowerment needed to overcome the obstacles because they have decided to exclude Jesus Christ out from their life because they falsely believed that they could do this without God. They only visit the church on Easter, Mother's Day, Christmas, or when they are desperately in trouble and have no choice but to try God. They discover through actual experience that God is merciful and he is a strong deliverer. After their deliverance, they tend to forget what God has done and end up right back where they started. The unfulfilled life is not worth living!

What is more, the unfilled life is a perpetual existence of self-inflicted abuse. It is a life of flux and consistent starting over which leads to anxiety about one's place in the world. It is a constant wrestling with oneself in the dark part of one's being, pinning down the true part of who we are. This life causes pain, both emotionally and spiritually. Emotional and spiritual pain is the impetus of physical pain and abuse. The unfilled life is falling down the rabbit hole with no bottom in sight. It is grappling in the dark, stumbling over objects which are unseen or discerned. This type of existence is not living, and so many in society feel they are trapped in the unfilled life.

If you would like to examine your heart because a man's purpose has to be found in his or her heart, then answer these few questions. Purpose is like deep water so you can no longer pull from shallow water.

- What do you have your mind set on? _____
- What thoughts dominate your mind? Thoughts of God or thoughts of the world? _____

- Are you easily turned away from focusing on God and His plans?
  _____

- What do you often reflect on? _____
- What are you passionate about? _____
- Can you be honest and list your appetites? _____
- What brings you joy? _____
- What makes you angry? _____
- Do you have a conscience? Do you think about your moral life? _____
  _____
  _____

- Do you have a rebellious spirit? Are you full of pride? _____

  What are the imaginations of thoughts in your head? Do you live in false worlds? _____
  _____
  _____

For though we walk in the flesh, we do not war after the flesh: (For the weapons of our warfare *are* not carnal, but mighty through God to the pulling down of strong holds;) **Casting down imaginations**, and every high thing that exalteth itself against the knowledge of God, and bringing into captivity every **thought** to the obedience of Christ (2 Cor. 10:3–5 KJV, emphasis added)

In his third letter to the Corinthian church, Paul instructs the believers that even though we walk in this physical body, we war differently. We have spiritual weapons to fight a spiritual enemy whose deception is to get us to buy into false worlds—*imaginations*. We have to cast down these false worlds and bring them into the captivity of the obedience of the anointing one and his anointing. The apostle *per excellence* also writes, "And we know that all things work together for good to them that love God, to them who are the called according to *his* **purpose**" (Rom. 8:28 KJV, *emphasis added*). *All things work together if:*

> ➢ If you love God unconditionally.
> ➢ If you recognize and answer the call.
>> ○ The call to salvation/regeneration, ministry, and the call to preparation!
> ➢ If you discover that your calling must be in harmony with God's purpose.
>> ○ You seek to know God's purpose and discern his will!

> For I know the thoughts that I think toward you, saith the LORD, thoughts of peace, and not of evil, to give you an expected end (Jer. 29:11 KJV).

A purpose driven life is about the expected end. It began the day you were born and will not be complete until your assignment in this life is completed and a pending grade from the Father of lights is given. You must seek God for his intentions to be revealed because his resulted aim determines your design and why you are thus. When you look at God's design in the mirror, it will take you on the journey of self-discovery, assessing your specifications and modifications that make you who you are. At that moment, a hunger will develop within because you are now ready to become what you are destined to become. You were born because God has a purpose for your life. The world needs your gifts, and only you can fulfill this God-given mission, which is your greater purpose. In sum, you will never be satisfied until you finally start living a purpose driven life.

1. What do you think God's intentions are for your life?

    _____

    _____

    _____

2. Why do you think God designed you the way he has?

    _____

    _____

    _____

3. Why do you love to do what you do?

    _____

    _____

    _____

4. Who benefits from what you love to do?

    _____

    _____

    _____

5. Do you find fulfillment in what you do?

    _____

    _____

    _____

6. If not, what should you be doing?

    _____

    _____

    _____

Reflection

Write your purpose statement.

_____

_____

_____

_____

_____

_____

_____

_____

_____

_____

_____

_____

_____

_____

_____

_____

_____

CHAPTER 5

Do You Know Your SHAPE?

A wise man *is* **strong**; yea, a man of knowledge increaseth **strength** (Prov. 24:5 KJV, emphasis added).

When thinking about your life and purpose, you will need to consider what *SHAPE* you are in. You must take self-inventory and know what condition your life is in. When one's life is out of *SHAPE*, it could be an indication of some damage that has been done to a life that has been wrongly handled. It can also be an indication of weakness or low vitality (i.e., living life without purpose). It is a life deemed unfit. There is a shortness of breath or the Holy Spirit active in the life of the person. Another important symptom of one who is out of *SHAPE* is a person with a bad heart condition.

Kevin Leman and William Pentak in *The Way of the Shepherd* give wise counsel to managers and leaders to always know the condition of their staff.[20] In this wisdom, they stated that *SHAPE* is an acronym for strengths, heart, attitude, personality, and experiences. In this book. they teach the Way of the Shepherd as a management technique in leading people. In the biblical sense of the word, a shepherd's responsibility is to lead and feed the flock. The shepherd also must not ignore a very important principle in leading the flock, the sheep of their pasture. A shepherd must know the *SHAPE* of their sheep. They have their shepherd's crook, which is the extension of

---

[20] Dr. Kevin Leman and William Pentak, *The Way of the Shepherd* (Grand Rapids: Zondervan, 2004), pp. 29–38.

their authority to keep the sheep in line. It is used when a sheep attempts to wander off, and the shepherd extends the crook to apprehend the ewe lamb to bring them back into the fold. This is important because if a sheep leaves the fold, it is in danger of becoming casted. In other words, the sheep can develop a sense of distrust or have a negative experience leading to a dispiriting effect. The shepherd's rod is a stick about five to six feet long, used by the pastor to protect and/or handle the sheep against its adversaries. It is the manager's responsibility to know the condition of his or her staff to be an effective leader. It is equally important for you to know your *SHAPE* as the steward over your life.

The genre of the scripture above is wisdom literature using Hebrew poetry with a chiastic expression. The writer of Proverbs asserts that a wise *man*, one who acquires the skill set to live well, is *strong*. The Hebrew word of choice is *geḇer*, which is translated as *man*. It connotes the kind of *man* who is a warrior. This is the kind of person who defends women and children or those who cannot fight for themselves. This Hebrew word hints at the nature of the man and is not gender-specific. This essence has overtones of spiritual strength, an inner wielding of sheer might. Zechariah the prophet, in chapter 7 verse 13, is giving a prophetic oracle about the Day of the Lord. In his oracle, he describes the shepherd as a man (*geḇer*) who stands next to the Lord God. The writer of the book of Job pens, "Can a man [*geḇer*] be profitable unto God, as he that is wise may be profitable unto himself?" (Job 22:2, KJV, *emphasis added*). Do you have a warrior's ability to overcome obstacles, setbacks, and intimate betrayal? If you do, you will be beneficial to God and to yourself. It is your inner strength that makes you not just a *man* but a warrior on *Yahweh's* strategic battle plan against the forces of darkness. You must be a warrior when considering your life strategy.

The second clause only reinforces the first by expounding that a wise *geḇer* is a man of knowledge. In order to be a possessor of knowledge, one has to have their eyes opened by the Spirit of God. He or she must hear God's voice when he is speaking. They must know how God speaks through his self-communication or revelation. God speaks through his word (Bible), prayer, circumstances, and through the five-fold ministry or those operating in the spiritual gifts. It is when one's eyes have been opened and they hear from God that they acquire knowledge (*da' ath*).

> He hath said, which heard the words of God, and knew the **knowledge** of the most High, *which* saw the vision of the Almighty, falling *into a trance*, but having his eyes open. (Num. 24:16, KJV)

It is in the wise man's pursuit of knowledge of God that he or she gains knowledge of self in order that one may grow in strength. In order to be considered a person of knowledge, you must chronicle your strengths, know what you are passionate about, survey your attitude, become aware of your personality (what type of spirit rules you), and appreciate your life experiences. The old sage writes again, "He that *hath* no rule over his own **spirit** *is like* a city *that is* broken down, *and* without walls" (Prov. 25:28 KJV, *emphasis added*). When reflecting on what condition your life is in, you have to know whether you rule over your own human spirit or is something else leading you.

If you don't rule over your spirit, some supernatural entity will come against you to take over. There is our human spirit that will attempt to subdue you by getting you to worship the shrine of your own opinion. There are evil spirits that will try to oppress you by distracting you from your purpose. A blood-washed born-again believer cannot be possessed, but they can be oppressed. Next, there is the Holy Spirit that lives inside of every believer. The Holy Spirit is gentle like the wind and will not override your human will (or human spirit) but will be a counselor to you. Case in point, you have to be willing to surrender to the Holy Spirit by stating as Jesus did "not my will but your will be done!" (Matt. 26:39).

Let's survey the sacred teaching narrative about the twelfth judge (or deliverer) named Samson in the book of Judges. He allowed the spirit of Delilah to get him to reveal his *heart*; thus, the secret of his *strength* was unveiled. It was his poor *attitude*, commanding *personality*, and lack of remembering his life *experiences* that caused his downfall. It was the spirit of Delilah that Samson allowed to rule over him which caused him to leave his heart exposed. Solomon, the wise one, wrote, "Keep thy heart with all diligence; for out of it *are* the issues of life" (Prov. 4:23 KJV). Always remember that the enemy will be lying in the shadows, intertwined in the crowd, and eavesdropping on your conversations to discover the secret of your heart; thereby, seeking the secret of your strength to ensnare you.

Strengths

> And it came to pass afterward, that he **loved** a woman in the valley of Sorek, whose name *was* Delilah. And the lords of the Philistines came up unto her, and said unto her, **Entice** him, and **see wherein his great strength** *lieth*, and **by what** *means* **we may prevail against him**, that we may bind him to afflict him: and we will give thee every one of us eleven hundred *pieces* of silver. And Delilah said **to Samson, Tell me, I pray thee, wherein thy great strength** *lieth*, and wherewith thou mightest be bound to afflict thee. (Judg. 16:4–6 KJV, emphasis added)

Strength is a thing alluding to the value or quality of being strong or capable. It is the source of one's ability to do a particular thing whether defined or undefined. It can also be the epicenter of one's capacity to endure the barrage of outside forces coming against their person or personality. When one possesses strength, they have the power to execute their sheer will. When one reflects on their strengths, it reveals a certain toughness that they may have, as well as an intensity to survive and thrive. Identifying your strengths allows you to initiate the force necessary to overcome and to accomplish your purpose. Do you know the degree of strength needed to win the battle, or reach the finish line of your long, sometimes circuitous journey? Assessing your strengths will assist you in discovering the things you do well and to evaluate your breaking point. Every person has a breaking point, and it will behoove you to know yours as you plan your life strategy. Your breaking point can be relationships with the opposite sex, family, your career, or whatever is precious to you. It is at your breaking point where the enemy will squeeze and apply the pressure to break you. However, the adversary did not make you; therefore, he cannot break you. He was to take advantage of the ones who do not know where their strength lies and trick them into self-destruction. Let's survey the narrative about Samson.

Samson or (*Shamshon*), meaning "like the sun," was born with a purpose. His mother was barren and had no children, then one day the angel of the Lord visited her and announced that she would bear a son who will be God's chosen vessel to deliver his people from the power of their enemies. You have to keep in mind always that you were born for a purpose and with a destiny. God has placed gifts inside of you that are needed in the generation in which you were born. Someone in your orbit needs your gifts (Acts 17:26). When Samson's mother told his father of the annunciation, he immediately wanted to confirm God's instructions on how Samson was to be raised. The angel of the Lord reiterated to the father and mother that Samson's birth was the work of God. His life was to be a vow to God, a Nazirite. He was appointed and anointed by God for a purpose. Knowing your *SHAPE* will help you discover your anointing and equip you to walk into your *port of call*.

The secret of Samson's strength did not lie in his pulchritude because it would not have been such a mystery to his adversaries where his great strength came from. It was not his biceps, triceps, and pectoralis (chest muscles). His strength was not conspicuous, or his enemies would have known how to defeat him. His strength was the Spirit of the living God coming upon him that gave him the fortitude to overcome his opponents. His seven locks were outward signs of God's inner grace and represented his commitment to God's purpose. Moses writes, "Speak unto the children of Israel, and say unto them, when either man or woman shall separate *themselves* to vow a vow of a **Nazarite**, to separate *themselves* unto the LORD" (Num. 6:2). What vows have you made to the Lord? Have you or are you keeping those commitments? What outwards signs do you have showing that you are consecrated and sanctified unto the Lord? Paul writes to the church that "we are more than conquerors through him who love us" (Rom. 8:37). Your opposition is constantly trying to discover the source of your inner strength. There are many blood-washed, tongue-talking, Bible-packing, praising the Lord saints who will tell you, "I don't look like what I been through!"

In the sacred text above, Samson had been successful in thwarting the enemies of God's people until he loved a woman who would eventually be the cause of his demise. The scriptures say, "He loved a woman in the valley of Sorek, whose name was Delilah." *Deliylah* (or Delilah) was a Philistine, and her name means "feeble." John Walton in *Ancient Near Eastern Thought and the Old Testament* helps us to understand in the Hebrew Bible that a name was important. When something or someone came into existence, it or they were given a name and a function (purpose). The name gave identity and framed the person's existence.[21] By the prophecy that is cryptic in Delilah's name reveals that she was the kind of woman that could bring a strong man to his knees and render him decrepit or feeble. The key to her plot to weaken Samson was to get him to reveal his heart, his innermost thoughts about himself, and his mission, which would allow the enemy to overtake him. Samson developed an ungodly soul tie with Delilah, which weakened him to reveal his secret.

Samuel writes that Samson loved Delilah. The Hebrew word used here is *aḥaḇ* (*aw-hav*), which has a semantic range of loving objects, people, or God. So when translating it under the auspices of the Holy Spirit, we must look at the context. It is possible that Samson had the kind of love for Delilah a man has for a wife. But on the contrary, *aḥaḇ* can be the kind of love that is carnal or a lustful desire (*libido*). After all, in the preceding periscope, Samson had come into Gaza and had relations with a prostitute. Nevertheless, he had an ungodly soul tie with Delilah. A soul tie is an emotional bond or connection that binds one person to another. It is a spiritual connection between a person you become intimate with or "become one

---

[21] John H. Walton, *Ancient Near Eastern Thought and the Old Testament* (Grand Rapids: Baker Academic, 2006), p. 92.

flesh" (Gen. 2:24). There are godly soul ties as well as ungodly ones. Samson developed an ungodly soul tie with Delilah, and it cost him his life. Ungodly soul ties are minions of the adversary which can sap your strength and render you powerless.

Ahab is that type of love that captures your soul and takes over your thought life. The Septuagint (LXX), which is the Greek Old Testament, translates the Hebrew word *ahab* as the Greek word *agapaō*, which can be rendered as a love based on evaluation and choice. The enemy knows your appetite or just what you like to attempt to draw you away. You hold the person in high regard, and you give them your loyalty, which is all variables of an ungodly soul tie. You strive for them constantly because you delight in them and abandon your objectives which are the milestones to you fulfilling your mission. You think about this person all the time and want to spend as much time with them as possible. Furthermore, it is the kind of love that causes you to think about the object of your affection more than your mission where your inner strength has now been compromised. When this happens, you become distracted, and your narrowed focus on your mission is in jeopardy. However, God used Samson's weakness to his advantage. God knows us better than we know ourselves, and there is nothing about us that surprises God. This is where Samson began to lose sight of his purpose.

In verse 5, Samson's enemies discover where his affection lies and discovered what was precious to him, which led to the investigation about his strength. The enemy asked Delilah to use beguilement and to seduce him in order to extract the information needed to defeat him and end his special assignment against them. The adversary did this over three thousand years ago with Samson, and he will attempt to do this to you in this season of your life. As you take inventory of your life, ask the question, Is there any beguiling going on or seducing to keep you on lock in a relationship in which you are unequally yoked (2 Cor. 6:14)? It is important to take note that Samson's strength did not lie in his appearance. In other words, Samson was not built like Arnold Schwarzenegger or a body builder because it would have been obvious where his strength lies. The Hebrew word for strength is *koach* (ko'-akh), which can be rendered as human strength, vigor, or efficiency. Samson's *koach* was dependent upon his inner vigor, which came from the Spirit of God. Much like Samson, people are trying to figure you out and discern where your inner strength comes from. They will underestimate you and misunderstand you because they wonder where your strength lies. Knowing your strengths is the first thing to be aware of in knowing what condition your life is in and assessing your *SHAPE*. Your strengths reveal your skill set or expertise.

Heart

> For where your treasure is, there will your **heart** be also (Matt. 6:21 KJV).

The next step in the process of teaching you your *SHAPE* is to assess your heart condition. An unhealthy heart is symptomatic of being out of shape. In order to assess your heart condition, you will have to describe your subjective complaints. Where is your pain or discomfort? What symptoms do you exhibit? What life event has killed your dream? What has arrested your passion? Consequently, we must run some tests so that we can discover the objective findings to give an assessment or diagnosis. Is it a toxic relationship that has fractured your heart and made you a permanent resident of Heartbreak Hotel? Is it the loss of someone dear to you? Is it failure? Have you failed at something in which you stepped out on faith and it did not work out as you expected? Finally, we must forecast or give a prognosis of the shape of your heart. Your heart will tell you what you are passionate about and where your focus lies. For example, where you spend your money is definitely an indicator to determine what is really important to you. Jesus made it plain in the scripture above, "…where your treasure is…"

Attitude

> And she said unto him, How canst thou say, I love thee, when thine heart *is* not with me? thou

hast mocked me these three times, and hast not told me wherein thy great strength *lieth*. And it came to pass, when she pressed him daily with her words, and urged him, *so* that his soul was vexed unto death; That he told her all his heart, and said unto her, There hath not come a razor upon mine head; for I *have been* a Nazarite unto God from my mother's womb: if I be shaven, then my strength will go from me, and I shall become weak, and be like any *other* man. (Judg. 16:15–17 KJV)

In her attempt to get Samson to reveal his secret, he mocked her three times. But she was relentless in getting the information out of him. Delilah had a can-do attitude. Even though Samson played her three times, she did not let that stop her because she set her mind on getting what she wanted—eleven hundred pieces of silver. An attitude is a way of thinking. A person's attitude will determine how far they will go in this life. Your attitude is affected by your thought life. Everything begins with a thought. Your thought life affects your words, feelings, and your actions. It is a viewpoint and can help or hinder your vision. Samson not giving her the answers she sought did not alter Delilah's temper or her approach. She was inclined to accomplish her mission by accomplishing the first objective: get Samson to tell her his heart. Your attitude reflects your perspective on the matter or positive thinking. It is because of her bodacious effort that Delilah ended up getting what she wanted. What made Delilah successful was her mind-set concerning her objective, her belief that she was good enough to extract the information from Samson, and her viewpoint of the object of her mission. Delilah had the right attitude. What is your mind-set regarding your life? What is your viewpoint on your mission? What do you really believe?

I can do all things through Christ which strengtheneth me (Phil. 4:13 KJV).

Personality

> And she made him sleep upon her knees; and she
> called for a man, and she caused him to shave
> off the seven locks of his head; and she began
> to afflict him, and his strength went from him.
> (Judg. 16:19 KJV)

Samson's heart was in Delilah's lap, and it was the beginning of his downfall. It was her personality that helped her accomplish her overall goal—the downfall of the mighty Samson. She had the temperament or makeup to do what no other woman could accomplish. It was her persona that got Samson to tell his heart by becoming vulnerable and letting his guard down. Delilah was an extrovert and had the charisma to seduce Samson to give her the key to his heart. It was her magnetism which drew Samson to her in that he knew that she was trying to get information from him that could destroy him, but he could not pull away. Delilah's personality type is the kind that is people-focused. When Samson came her way, she narrowed her focus on him and would not let it go. She was charismatic and knew how to connect with him. She was a Philistine, and he was an Israelite. That did not stop the connection she had made with him. She was focused on what she could do with the money she would gain by betraying Samson instead on the reality of her current situation.

It is imperative that you know your personality type. Learning your personality is about knowing your makeup. Are you an extrovert or introvert? Are you shy or outgoing? Are you the life of the party, or would you prefer to be at home reading a book or watching your favorite show? Do you thrive in change or do you hate change? These are just a few questions you must answer as you assess your *SHAPE*. Delilah had the right personality to accomplish her mission. Do you have the right personality to accomplish yours? Another way of looking at personality is asking if you have the right spirit for the task at hand. This is crucial when developing your life strategy.

Experiences

Have you ever heard that you are a product of your environment? The correct way to put this sentiment is that you are an end result of your life experience whether positive or negative. Your experiences shape you in ways that you cannot imagine. They can also be an impetus that drives you to become the person you desire. As you begin to seek and understand you purpose and develop your life strategy, reflect on your life experiences. Delilah's life experiences made her the perfect candidate for God to use to get Samson in the place to destroy more enemies in his death than he did while he was alive.

> And Samson called unto the LORD, and said, O Lord GOD, remember me, I pray thee, and strengthen me, I pray thee, only this once, O God, that I may be at once avenged of the Philistines for my two eyes. And Samson took hold of the two middle pillars upon which the house stood, and on which it was borne up, of the one with his right hand, and of the other with his left. And Samson said, Let me die with the Philistines. And he bowed himself with *all his* might; and the house fell upon the lords, and upon all the people that *were* therein. So the dead which he slew at his death were more than *they* which he slew in his life (Judg. 16:28–30 KJV).

Delilah was a very attractive woman who probably had to deal with men coming on to her since her early youth. She developed the charm and magnetism to manipulate men to get what she wanted out of them. It was not just her pulchritude, but she had to learn how to talk to a man and how to ask the questions to get the desired information. Her mother possibly was her mentor in her development, and she could have seen her mother at work doing the same thing. It was her positive and negative life experiences that caused Delilah to be used by God in order that his will would be accomplished.

How do you view your life experiences? Have you chronicled them whether positive or negative in a journal? Do you see your negative life experiences as a catalyst to motivate you to do better and overcome all the odds against your life's success? Do you use your positive life experiences as a reminder that you are a warrior? Write down your life experiences and scan the positive and negative ones to rewrite your story. This is needed to know your *SHAPE*.

What SHAPE are you in?

Use the lists of strengths and weaknesses to chart your *SHAPE*. Use the same lists to put together a *SWOT* (strengths, weaknesses, opportunities, and threats) analysis for your life.

What are your **S**trengths? _____

_____

What are you passionate about? What's in your **H**eart? _____

_____

What type of **A**ttitude do you have? _____

_____

Do you know what kind of **P**ersonality you possess? _____

_____

List your **E**xperiences—both good and bad, positive or negative—that have *shaped you*.

_____

_____

_____

_____

_____

_____

_____

_____

_____

_____

_____

SWOT Analysis

Strengths: _____

_____

_____

Weaknesses: _____

_____

_____

Opportunities: _____

_____

_____

Threats: _____

_____

_____

List of Strengths

Accuracy	Entertaining	Logical
Action-oriented	Enthusiastic	Love
Adventurous	Fair	Love of learning
Ambitious	Fast	Mercy
Analytical	Flexible	Modesty
Appreciative	Focused	Motivation
Artistic	Forceful	Observant
Athletic	Friendliness	Optimistic
Caring	Generosity	Open-minded
Clever	Gratitude	Orderly
Compassionate	Honesty	Originality
Charm	Hope	Organization
Communicative	Humility	Outgoing
Confident	Humor	Patient
Considerate	Honesty	Perseverance
Courage	Idealism	Persuasiveness
Creativity	Independence	Persistence
Critical thinking	Ingenuity	Practical
Curiosity	Industriousness	Precise
Dedication	Inner peace	Problem-solving
Determination	Inspirational	Prudence
Discipline	Integrity	Respect
Dedication	Intelligence	Responsibility
Educated	Kindness	Self-assurance
Empathetic	Knowledgeable	Seriousness
Energetic	Leadership	Self-control

List of Strengths Continued

Spirituality	Evaluating	Proofreading
Spontaneous	Examining	Prioritizing
Social intelligence	Explaining	Questioning
Social skills	Editing	Qualifying
Straightforward	Empowering	Researching
Strategic thinking	Fixing	Resolving
Tactful	Formulating	Reporting
Team oriented	Finalizing	Recording
Thoughtful	Guiding a group or individual	Repairing
Thrifty	Gathering information	Reviewing
Tolerant	Generating ideas	Scheduling
Trustworthy	Giving feedback	Selling
Versatile	Helping	Supervising
Visionary	Handling	Simplifying
Vitality	Hosting	Speaking
Warmth	Imagining	Strategizing
Willpower	Implementing	Teaching
Workplace Strengths	Influencing	Teamwork
Adapting	Initiating	Troubleshooting
Administering	Innovating	Training
Analyzing	Interviewing	Tracking details
Arranging	Instructing	Thinking creatively
Advising	Judging	Understanding
Budgeting	Learning	Uniting
Building teams	Listening	Upgrading
Briefing	Locating	Updating

Balancing	Launching	Verbalizing
Communicating	*Leading*	*Volunteering*
Controlling	Managing	Verifying
Coordinating	Mentoring	Writing
Creating	Monitoring	
Checking	Motivating	
Counseling	Marketing	
Compiling	Negotiating	
Coaching	Navigating	
Deciding	Organizing	
Detailing	Overhauling	
Developing people	Overseeing	
Directing	Persuading	
Devising	Planning	
Discovering	Preparing	
Data input	Presenting	
Empathizing	Problem-solving	

General Strengths of Leaders and Managers

Communication Strengths	Make objectives and outcomes specific
Clear and concise in verbalizing ideas	Clearly communicate objectives and outcomes
Allow effective communication	Able to fully explain tasks and delegate them
Able to summarize and clarify	Create and provide clear standards and expectations
Actively listen to ideas	Develop checks and controls
Give constructive criticism	Oversee staff to keep them on task

Take time to make a personal connection	Strengths for supporting staff
Strengths for providing direction	Know talents of workers in order to delegate effectively
Communication Strengths	Make objectives and outcomes specific
Clearly communicate objectives and outcomes	Strengths for supporting staff
Able to fully explain tasks and delegate them	Know talents of workers in order to delegate effectively
Create and provide clear standards and expectations	Provide staff training and development
Develop checks and controls	Empower workers by delegating some responsibilities
Oversee staff to keep them on task	Evaluate staff performance on a regular basis
Clearly communicate objectives and outcomes	Recognize efforts of workers

List of Weaknesses

Not taking criticism well	Stubborn
Impatient	Multitasking
Lazy	Allows emotions to show
Easily bored	Blunt
Procrastinate	Presenting
Persistent	Impulsive
Takes things personally	Bossy
Strong willed	Takes on too much
Passive	Follow-ups
Does not like conflict	Aggressive
Shy	Likes to take risks

Lethargic	Critical of others
Long-term planning	Passive
Strict	Works too much
Shortsighted	Perfectionist
Selfish	Fearful
Focusing on small details	Self critic
Takes blame for others	Trouble with teams
Being straightforward	Close-minded
Greedy	Unorganized
Delegating tasks	Does not like pressure
Needs to be right	

CHAPTER 6

Discovering My Divinely Ordained Mission

And he came to Nazareth, where he had been brought up: and, as his custom was, he went into the synagogue on the sabbath day, and stood up for to read. And there was delivered unto him the book of the prophet Esaias. And when he had opened the book, he found the place where it was written, The Spirit of the Lord *is* upon me, because he hath anointed me to preach the gospel to the poor; he hath sent me to heal the broken-hearted, to preach deliverance to the captives, and recovering of sight to the blind, to set at liberty them that are bruised, To preach the acceptable year of the Lord. And he closed the book, and he gave *it* again to the minister, and sat down. And the eyes of all them that were in the synagogue were fastened on him. And he began to say unto them, This day is this scripture fulfilled in your ears. And all bare him witness, and wondered at the gracious words which proceeded out of his mouth. And they said, Is not this Joseph's son? (Luke 4:16–22 KJV)

Have you ever planned a trip without consulting a map? Have you ever decided to get to a particular destination without a trip plan? Have you ever engaged in doing a particular task without questioning why you are doing it? Have you ever felt as if you were aimlessly meandering through life—just simply existing? If you answered yes to the first and second question, then you can expect some unforeseen problems to come along, even the possibility of getting lost. If you answered yes to the third question, you probably stopped the activity because it was a waste of time. Finally, if you answer yes to the fourth question, then you have been simply living without a mission and devoid of purpose. It is when one knows their assignment when one becomes enthused to become animated to a cause of action that produces fulfillment or a sense of achievement. Having a sense of purpose or adding value to other peoples' lives in the world can be one way you can begin to scratch at the surface of your mission.

In Luke 4:16–22, Jesus is asked to perform the reading of the Law and the Prophets in the synagogue on the Sabbath. And after reading the word, he conveys his mission:

- to preach the gospel to the poor
- to heal the brokenhearted
- to preach deliverance to the captives
- to set at liberty to those who are oppressed
- help the blind to recover their sight
- to preach the Jubilee

He clarifies from the scripture that he was anointed for this very purpose, reading from the book of Isaiah. This story tradition in the Gospel according to Luke is a teaching narrative that instructs the believers that we must start with the Word in discerning our mission.

What Is My Mission?

Why is light given to a man whose way is hid, and whom God hath hedged in (Job 3:23 KJV)?

You have probably heard some speak of knowing their mission or seeking to find their mission in life. So what is a mission? Your mission is synonymous to your calling in life. By definition, a mission is a task one has been sent to accomplish. It is receiving *holy orders* from the Great Eternal Designer who purposed you to be here in this world and elected to have you come forth in your generation (Acts 17:26). You were born with a purpose and with particular gifts to be shared in the world around you. Your mission is a special kind of work that you were born to accomplish. Your mission is a purpose of life, and you must formulate a life strategy to go about the business of accomplishing the assignment which was given to you. Your mission is a message which is meant to communicate information encrypted in your life's journey to a target market or target audience that God has chosen just for you. Therefore, knowing you mission is so important. You need the information and specs to get your operation in order because you have been charged by a power higher than you to fulfill your duty to this world.

The verse above sits within the pericope Job 3:20–23, in which the author raises a rhetorical question: "Why does He give light to the sufferer and life to the bitter of soul?" This person waits for death, which he thinks is the cessation of life. This individual's only celebration and exuberation is in the destination of the grave. This describes the feelings of a person devoid of his or her mission or calling. In verse 23, the author highlights this is a strong man or a warrior *(geber)* whose mission or path is hidden, but God protects such a man by placing a hedge around him. The scripture speaks to those of us who are searching for that one thing that makes us feel alive because we feel like a fish out of water, desperately needing to breath. A fish was made for a particular ecosystem, and if it is outside of the environment it was meant to live in and strive in, it suffocates. But there is hope because God protects those whose mission is hidden. If you feel that your path is a mystery, which is a secret meant to be revealed at God's *kairos time,* then hold on until the light shines upon the path you are to take. Discovering your mission is vital to your life strategy.

> But he knoweth the way that I take: *when* he hath tried me, I shall come forth as gold. My foot hath held his steps, his way (**path**) have I kept, and not declined (Job 23:10–11 KJV, emphasis added).

Laurie Beth Jones educates her readers by etching in *The Path*, "It would be foolish to undertake such a mighty task as determining one's mission in life without first contemplating the overall scheme of things."[22] She points out that two important variables are necessary in envisaging your mission in life:

1. Meditating, which is the opportunity to think quietly, consider, and plan.
2. Reflecting has to do with careful thinking or strategic contemplation.

You must take time to meditate to some soaking prophetic music and listen for God to speak. As you take a moment to quiet your mind and reflect on what God has brought you through and where he is bringing you from, then it will become clear through the process of progressive revelation what your mission is. One must possess self-knowledge or know your *SHAPE* coupled with possession of self-esteem and self-determination to discern your mission and fulfill it. Jones makes a powerful acknowledgement expressing the importance of the reader, considering that their mission will be compatible with their **personality** or character traits.[23] Samuel the judge, prophet, and priest writes about how King Saul was rejected by God for not fulfilling the mission:

> And the LORD sent you on a mission and said, 'Go, devote to destruction the sinners, the Amalekites, and fight against them until they are consumed.' 1Why then did you not obey the

---

[22] Laurie Beth Jones, *The Path* (New York: ABC Publishing, 2003), pg. 23.
[23] IBID, pg. 25.

voice of the LORD? Why did you pounce on the spoil and do what was evil in the sight of the LORD?" And Saul said to Samuel, "I have obeyed the voice of the LORD. I have gone on the mission on which the LORD sent me. I have brought Agag the king of Amalek, and I have devoted the Amalekites to destruction. But the people took of the spoil, sheep and oxen, the best of the things devoted to destruction, to sacrifice to the LORD your God in Gilgal." And Samuel said, "Has the LORD as great delight in burnt offerings and sacrifices, as in obeying the voice of the LORD? Behold, to obey is better than sacrifice, and to listen than the fat of rams. For rebellion is as the sin of divination, and presumption is as iniquity and idolatry. Because you have rejected the word of the LORD, he has also rejected you from being king." (1 Sam. 15:18–23 ESV)

When confronted by the prophet, King Saul began to make excuses why he did not obey God's directives and complete his mission. He did start off on the right path, but he allowed greed and pride to override his conscious, which caused him to divert from his objectives. When planning your mission, remember that objectives are the stepping-stones that lead you to accomplishing your overall assignment from God. Saul forgot his overall commission by turning away from the aims which would have led him to the completion of his mission. Do you have a list of objectives to lead you to accomplishing your mission? *Hear this prophetic word, "Your charge is to accomplish your objectives in spite of what comes at you in order to complete your mission!"* Now you must discover the objectives to your mission.

The following step must be followed to accomplish your divinely appointed mission:

- You must have in mind (consciously or unconsciously) your overall assignment from God that you must achieve.

Let this mind be in you, which was also in Christ Jesus: Who, being in the form of God, thought it not robbery to be equal with God: But made himself of no reputation, and took upon him the form of a servant, and was made in the likeness of men: And being found in fashion as a man, he humbled himself, and became obedient unto death, even the death of the cross. Wherefore God also hath highly exalted him, and given him a name which is above every name: That at the name of Jesus every knee should bow, of *things* in heaven, and *things* in earth, and *things* under the earth; And *that* every tongue should confess that Jesus Christ *is* Lord, to the glory of God the Father.(Phil. 2:5–11 KJV)

- Take stock by doing an environmental scan. Who is in your orbit? Remove those who are praying and planning for your downfall!

Be ye not unequally yoked together with unbelievers: for what fellowship hath righteousness with unrighteousness? and what communion hath light with darkness? And what concord hath Christ with Belial? or what part hath he that believeth with an infidel? And what agreement hath the temple of God with idols? for ye are the temple of the living God; as God hath said, I will dwell in them, and walk in *them*; and I will be their God, and they shall be my people. Wherefore come out from among them, and be ye separate, saith the Lord, and touch not the unclean *thing*; and I will receive you, And will be a Father unto you, and ye shall be my sons and daughters, saith the Lord Almighty. (2 Cor. 6:14 KJV)

- Analyze your situation.
- List your goals.

The steps of a *good* man are ordered by the LORD: and he delighteth in his way. (Ps. 37:23 KJV)

- Formulate your strategy or list the activities to accomplish your goals.
- Develop your objectives or aims—the stepping-stones which will keep you on track to your destination.
- List the tasks, no matter how difficult, that you will need to do to be successful.
- Make a list of the resources needed. This includes people, materials, technologies, and money required to implement your strategy or processes.
- Develop a timeline.
- *Write the vision.*

I will stand upon my watch, and set me upon the tower, and will watch to see what he will say unto me, and what I shall answer when I am reproved. 2 And the LORD answered me, and said, Write the vision, and make *it* plain upon tables, that he may run that readeth it. 3 For the vision *is* yet for an appointed time, but at the end it shall speak, and not lie: though it tarry, wait for it; because it will surely come, it will not tarry. 4 Behold, his soul *which* is lifted up is not upright in him: but the just shall live by his faith (Hab. 2:1–4 KJV)

- Acknowledge and celebrate successes, small or great.

Remember, your goals must be specific, measurable, acceptable, and realistic. They must have a time frame, stretch you beyond your comfort zone, and be rewarding. You have to have a specific aim in mind. The prophet Habakkuk gives some very inspiring words to the people of God as he charges them to first stand watch. You are the watchman who stands guard over your life and the mission God has given you. You cannot blame or point the finger at no one for not fulfilling your destiny. You just have to know your destination and complete a trip plan. You have to stand watch and listen to what God is saying to you. Keep a journal or composition notebook by your bedside so when God speaks to your through dreams and visions, you can begin to write what he has shown you. In the historical narrative of sacred history, Luke records Peter's first expository sermon as he quotes Joel the prophet:

> But this is that which was spoken by the prophet Joel; And it shall come to pass in the last days, saith God, I will pour out of my Spirit upon all flesh: and your sons and your daughters shall prophesy, and **your young men shall see visions**, and **your old men shall dream dreams**: And on my servants and on my handmaidens I will pour out in those days of my Spirit; and they shall prophesy:(Acts 2:16–18 KJV, *emphasis added*)

The prophet lets us know that in the last days, God is going to pour out his spirit upon all human beings despite ethnicity, gender, socioeconomic, sociopolitical, or demographical status one might be classified. The result of this spiritual phenomenon is that those who receive his spirit will begin to speak by the divine inspiration of the Holy Spirit what God has shown them. They will utter what God has shown them through visions and through their dreams. Once you get the picture, you must write what you see. Adam Thompson and Adrian Beale in *The Divinity Code* define visions as "a vision is a revelation straight to the human spirit, a deposit from God injected into our spirits that interrupts soulish or conscious activity."[24] Thompson and Beale explains to the readers that dreams unveil the activities that

---

[24] Adam F. Thompson and Adrian Beale, *The Divinity Code* (Shippenburg: Destiny Image, 2011), pp. 82–83.

are taking place in the spirit realm and project through visual images these events to the natural person.[25] However, you need the Holy Spirit to discern the encrypted communication from God.

> But the natural man receiveth not the things of the Spirit of God: for they are foolishness unto him: neither can he know *them*, because they are spiritually discerned. (1 Cor. 2:14 KJV)

Are You Hearing What God Is Saying?

> For many are called, but few *are* chosen (Matt. 22:14 KJV)

There is an inner call of the Holy Spirit and the outer call which are the proofs of your calling recognized by the community in which you are invested. Your mission is your calling. It is being commissioned on special business with holy orders coming from God. Your calling is your purpose of life. It is when you become active as God's asset in the world and become fully engage in the work you have been training for and prepared for since you were born. You must become involved in your assignments and do the research as well as make the preparations. You don't have time to be slow about your activity and become distracted by those who are not meant to go where your calling is leading you. Your calling is not idle work. Even when you are in recess, God is behind the scenes working everything out for you good (Rom. 8:28).

> So he called ten of his servants, delivered to them ten minas, and said to them, 'Do **business** till I come (Luke 19:13 NKJ, emphasis added).

Jesus was teaching a valuable lesson in this parable, "Do business till I come!" Answering your calling is about being about your

---

[25] Thompson and Beal, *The Diviniy Code*, p. 29.

Father's business. It is being occupied with the work you have been assigned to do in this world. While engaged in your assignment, you will face difficulties and hardships. The parable teaches that at the consummation of history, you will have to give an account to God of what you did with the gifts and talents you were given. The chief question you will be asked is "Did you add any value to the world while you lived and existed during your generation?" Do you know the work that has been assigned to you? Do you have the particular details to your assignment?

Reflection

First, pray and fast, then below list what you believe to be your mission. Secondly, list some of your goals, objectives, and tasks you believe are necessary to accomplish your mission. Next, sketch a timeline for when you plan to implement your strategic plan and when you plan to accomplish your objectives. You are ready to write the vision that God is giving you.

What is my mission? _____

_____

_____

What are my goals? _____

What are the objectives needed to accomplish my goals? _____

_____

What are the tasks I need to do? _____

Write a timeline. _____

_____

Write the _vision_: _____

_____

_____

_____

_____

_____

_____

_____

_____

_____

_____

CHAPTER 7

Man, Know Thy Self

> When I was a child, I spake as a child, I under-
> stood as a child, I thought as a child: but when
> I became a man, I put away childish things. For
> now we see through a glass, darkly; but then face
> to face: now I know in part; but then shall I know
> even as also I am known (1 Cor. 13:11–12 KJV).

So Who Are You?

"Who am I?" is one of the most asked questions in the world and asked in almost every language known to man. In attempting to answer this question, most start with biology by focusing on his or her parents which is *bios*—the physical life. This is interesting because *bios,* where we get the word *biology,* is temporary. We naturally start with what we know to answer an eternal question because we cannot decipher what we do not know—the eternal. So we live our lives trying to accumulate temporary things because we only believe in a temporary life (*bios*). In our pursuit of happiness, we only find heartache and pain, disappointment and shame, only to be made aware that money and things cannot buy us happiness. The void is still there with an appetite that needs your undivided attention and needs to be fed. Who am I? Why am I thus? These inquiries are the most important queries you will ever pursue in your lifetime.

The scriptures above come from the love chapter in the book of First Corinthians. The scriptures fit within the pericope of 1 Corinthians 13:8–13, which begins with an exposition about love. Then the apostle does something different and unexpected by declaring, "When I was a child I spoke as a child..." The Greek word translated as "child" is *nēpios* (nay'-pee-os), which has several connotations. The essence of *nēpios* literally is an infant, figuratively of a person unspotted by the world and negatively of a childish person. It can speak of youthfulness, innocence, or immaturity. In order to find out who you are, you start with loving yourself enough to find out the truth about yourself. Self-knowledge is contingent upon self-love. People who do not possess self-love are dealing with self-hatred. These types of people don't care about finding out who they really are and are aimlessly traversing through life, accepting whatever the world has to offer them. They work mediocre jobs that are beneath their talent, and they ended up in relationships overcompensating for a person who was not called or meant to love them. The theologian *per excellence* concludes this expression by stating, "When I became a man I put away childish things!"

Paul is speaking of a progression of the development of the self. When one is unspotted in the world or in a state of innocence, his or her understanding is at base level. The scripture begins with the Greek word *hóte*, which is an adverb indicating linear time with a historical sense. "When I was a child [*nēpios*]I spoke [*laléō*] as a child..." When one is immature or maybe even naïve, the person can only express himself or herself on the level of their thinking. This in turn allows one to only reason based on their limited experience which is due to their lack of conventional wisdom which is accumulated through life experiences coupled with their lack of divine wisdom which only comes from God. The indigenous elders on the continent of Africa, teachers in *Mystery Systems*, charged those seeking a higher level of thinking to know themselves. Self-knowledge is a journey that begins with one step. The apostle continues by stating, "...when I became a man..." At this clause, he make a reference of linear time to highlight the progression from a child (*nēpios*) to a man (*anēr*), which is "a man of mature understanding as opposed to a child (1 Cor. 13:11, Eph.

4:13)."[26] In other words, the individual who grows in love begins to transition from a lower level of understanding to a higher level as long as they are seeking knowledge of self. When a person begins to mature, they put away their childish thinking because they can handle more complex concepts or situations and think logically regarding the new information that is now in their possession.

In verse 12, the apostle states the obvious: "For now we see through a mirror in an enigma..." The Greek word translated as "darkly" in the KJV, "poor reflection" in the NIV, "dimly" in the ESV, and "imperfectly" in the NLT is *aínigma*. The literal translation is enigma or riddle. When it comes to learning to know oneself, the journey begins as a riddle or a mysterious thing. James Fadiman and Robert Frager in *Personality & Personal Growth* states, "The self is an elusive concept, never completely captured by any of the theorists. It is more than the ego, more than the sum total of factors that make up the individual; it is less limited than the personality but contains it."[27] However, as the individual moves close to the mirror (*ésoptron*), which is a piece of flat metal polished to reflect an image, the more his or her true image is manifest from a base level to a higher level, ultimately revealing the true self. The reflection of the self being manifested is both physical and spiritual. As one continues on the journey of self-knowledge, the person goes from knowing in part to full knowledge of self as God reveals to the individual who they truly are. In sum, our knowledge of self is intricately tied to knowledge of God.

Ra Un Nefer Amen in his book *Metu Neter Vol. 1* speaks of the duality of being and defines what is the true *self*. He equates the self with true consciousness. He avers that we don't just have consciousness, but we are consciousness, which is the *self*. This consciousness is non-energy matter; it is a matter of the will. Consciousness is not the mind, but it is awareness or a knowing. The object of knowledge is understanding; thereby, knowledge also can be a function of perception. What do you perceive about yourself? Ra Un Nefer Amen

---

[26] *avnh, r, The Complete Word Study Dictionary New Testament*, Spiros Zodhiates, Ed. (Chattanooga: AMG, 1993), p. 172.

[27] James Fadiman and Robert Frager, *Personality & Personal Growth* (Upper Saddle River: Prentice Hall, 1974), p. 11.

asserts that perception recognizes. So perception coupled with recognition produces knowledge. What do you recognize about yourself? Do you recognize that you are consciousness? It is when you recognize you are consciousness, then you will discover that recognition of consciousness is true identity.

> My people are destroyed for lack of knowledge: because thou hast rejected knowledge, I will also reject thee, that thou shalt be no priest to me: seeing thou hast forgotten the law of thy God, I will also forget thy children (Hosea 4:6 KJV)

In the eighth century, before the Common Era, Hosea the prophet was given an assignment to prophesy to God's people about their current situation. Things were going well, and the people had become unfaithful and forgot their God. When this happened, God deployed his servant, the prophet Hosea, to give the people a most important message. My people ('ammī) are cut off because they lack knowledge of me and my ways because they have rejected my instructions through knowledge. This is a great cost to them because I will reject them and their children because of their ignorance of me and my ways. Without my knowledge, you cannot represent me to the people, nor can you represent the people to me. I will reject your prayers and your sacrifices because you have forgotten my *tōrah (law)*. John Calvin wrote in *the Institutes of Christian Religion,* "Nearly all wisdom which we possess, that is to say, true and sound wisdom, consists of two parts: the knowledge of God and of ourselves. But, while joined by many bonds, which one precedes and brings forth the other, is not easy to discern." Calvin is confused because he does not know if knowledge of self preceded the knowledge of God or vise versa. It is my presupposition that knowledge of God comes first to usher one in the true knowledge of self. However, we can become devoid of the knowledge of self if we reject the knowledge God has given.

When one forgets his or her creator, that person will experience intimate betrayals, family relationship disintegration, failed friendships, and loss knowledge of self. Self-destruction is inevitable when a person loses sight of purpose and awareness of who God created them to be. After all, it is commonly known that your *being* flows out of your *doing*. Hosea warns the people of God that they are destroyed because they lack knowledge. They lack the important information and revelation which gives them an understanding of their current situation. One cannot grasp the meaning of life without knowledge. A person cannot have a sense of purpose without understanding. According to the prophet, the people's dilemma is a result of their rejection of knowledge. One then must go deeper and ask, "Why would a person reject knowledge?"

In the temples throughout the Nile Valley and at the University of Timbuktu in the country of Mali in West Africa, the African wise men encouraged the new disciples that he or she must know themselves on their path to enlightenment—the task of learning the skill sets of living well. One cannot know themselves intimately without knowing their parents and grandparents who preceded them. Most importantly, one cannot truly know themselves without the spiritual phenomenon we call God. Jones brings up another import variable in seeking God to learn your mission in life. You must become aware of the personalities that influenced you from the past. These are people, such as parents, teachers, mentors, or leaders, who have had a positive or negative influence on you growing up. Jones recites a quote from renowned psychiatrist Carl Jung that "Nothing affects the environment of a child so much as the unlived life of a parent." [28] In discerning your mission, take time to reflect on the personality influences from your past and your parents' "*unlived lives.*"

Who is your biggest influence from your past?

    a. mother/father
    b. grandmother/father
    c. aunt/uncle
    d. teacher/mentor
    e. other: _____

[28] Laurie Beth Jones, *The Path* (New York: ABC Publishing, 2003), pg. 34.

Luke gives us a description of Saul of Tarsus before he became Paul the apostle of Jesus Christ who was the greatest missionary of all time. We learn from Luke's historical narrative that Saul's personality influence was one of the greatest teachers in Jerusalem—Gamaliel. So we can deduce that Saul learned to have a zeal for the law from watching Gamaliel, his teacher. He was studious and pious and serious about his studies by mirroring his teacher, Gamaliel.

> I am verily a man *which am* a Jew, born in Tarsus, *a city* in Cilicia, yet brought up in this city at the feet of Gamaliel, *and* taught according to the perfect manner of the law of the fathers, and was zealous toward God, as ye all are this day (Acts 22:3 KJV).

> Then stood there up one in the council, a Pharisee, named Gamaliel, a doctor of the law, had in reputation among all the people, and commanded to put the apostles forth a little space (Acts 5:34 KJV).

He also learned to be legalistic and judgmental from his personality influence. He stood and watched Stephen being stoned to death because of the worldview he learned from his mentor. In order to stand idly by and watch a human being murdered, one would have to be cold, heartless, and narcissistic.

> Then they cried out with a loud voice, and stopped their ears, and ran upon him with one accord, And cast *him* out of the city, and stoned *him*: and the witnesses laid down their clothes at a young man's feet, whose name was Saul (Acts 7:57–58 KJV).

It was not until Saul was converted and accepted Jesus Christ into his heart did he have an opportunity to reflect upon his actions and the influence of his mentor on him at that time in his life. But when he answered the call of Jesus Christ, he began to see himself as God saw him. He began to gain knowledge of self; he became the great missionary of all time.

> For ye have heard of my conversation in time past in the Jews' religion, how that beyond measure I persecuted the church of God, and wasted it: And profited in the Jews' religion above many my equals in mine own nation, being more exceedingly zealous of the traditions of my fathers. But when it pleased God, who separated me from my mother's womb, and called *me* by his grace, To reveal his Son in me, that I might preach him among the heathen; immediately I conferred not with flesh and blood: Neither went I up to Jerusalem to them which were apostles before me; but I went into Arabia, and returned again unto Damascus (Gal. 1:13 KJV).

Another example of the importance of the personality influence in one's life is Mary and Elizabeth. During the Annunciation, when Mary was given her assignment to be the *theotokos* or the mother of God, she was in disbelief. She had a hard time accepting that she was chosen to be the God carrier because she lacked the experience and the know-how. As a result of her perplexity, the angel Gabriel referred her to her personality influence. Elizabeth was able to relate to Mary's plight because she was barren, but she had a husband. She was able to share her testimony of the impossible. She was living proof that God still worked miracles in the lives of his people. Mary began to discover that she was more than a teenage girl from a small village. She gained knowledge of self to become the mother of the son of God.

> Then said Mary unto the angel, How shall this be, seeing I know not a man? And the angel answered and said unto her, The Holy Ghost shall come upon thee, and the power of the Highest shall

overshadow thee: therefore also that holy thing
which shall be born of thee shall be called the
Son of God. And, behold, thy cousin Elisabeth,
she hath also conceived a son in her old age: and
this is the sixth month with her, who was called
barren. For with God nothing shall be impossible. And Mary said, Behold the handmaid of the
Lord; be it unto me according to thy word. And
the angel departed from her (Luke 1:34–38 KJV).

Mary took the advice of the angel Gabriel and went to visit
Elizabeth herself. After her visit and shared experience with her mentor, Mary was ready to deal with the challenges, setbacks, and criti-
cism of others as she was determined to fulfill her mission.

And Mary arose in those days, and went into the
hill country with haste, into a city of Juda; 40
And entered into the house of Zacharias, and
saluted Elisabeth. 41 And it came to pass, that,
when Elisabeth heard the salutation of Mary, the
babe leaped in her womb; and Elisabeth was filled
with the Holy Ghost: 42 And she spake out with
a loud voice, and said, Blessed *art* thou among
women, and blessed *is* the fruit of thy womb. 43
And whence *is* this to me, that the mother of my
Lord should come to me? 44 For, lo, as soon as
the voice of thy salutation sounded in mine ears,
the babe leaped in my womb for joy. 45 And
blessed *is* she that believed: for there shall be a
performance of those things which were told her
from the Lord (Luke 1:39–45 KJV).

Reflection

1. If asked, how would you answer the question, "Who are you?" _____

2. Do you love yourself? If so, what is the love of self? _____

3. Write down in your journal your path to self-discovery. What is your current station on your journey? _____ _____

4. Can you identify the moment you recognized you change and moved to another level? Explain. _____ _____

5. When you look into the mirror, what do you see? _____ _____

6. Has your consciousness been awakened? _____ _____

CHAPTER 8

Your Spiritual Gifts

> Now there are diversities of gifts, but the same
> Spirit. And there are differences of administrations,
> but the same Lord. And there are diversities of
> operations, but it is the same God which worketh
> all in all. But the manifestation of the Spirit is given
> to every man to profit withal (1 Cor. 12:4–7 KJV).

A significant part of your life strategy is discovery your spiritual gifts.
Why? Spiritual gifts are necessary for pursuing life of power which
will enhance both your emotional and physical life. They are evidence that a believer has been baptized in the Holy Spirit. The lack of
knowledge of the *charismata* is self-evident of a powerless church. Are
you seeking answers to some of the most profound questions on your
journey? The spiritual gifts such as a word of wisdom and knowledge
can remedy the pain you feel. When you are pursuing your life dream
and you find yourself in a hard place, a prophetic word can build
you up, draw you near, and console you. When you are in need of
emotional, spiritual, or physical healing, the gifts of healings will be
beneficial to your hurting soul. Even leadership and generosity are
spiritual gifts (Rom. 12:8).

After reflecting on your knowledge of self, ordained mission,
and personal personalities who influenced you, you must turn your
attention to discerning what spiritual gifts (*charismata*) (*kha-ris-
măh-ta*) you possess. *Nelson's Illustrated Bible Dictionary* defines them

as "special gifts bestowed by the Holy Spirit upon Christians for the purpose of building up the church."[29] Spiritual gifts are not the same as natural talents and abilities. Natural talents and abilities can include but not be limited to physical strength, intelligence, artistic abilities, and managerial skillfulness. John MacArthur observed, "Spiritual gifts are not talents. Natural talents, skills, and abilities are granted by God just as everything good and worthwhile is a gift from Him. But those things are natural abilities shared by believers and unbelievers alike."[30] A person may have a talent to be an athlete but do not need the endowment of the Holy Spirit to dunk a basketball or score a touchdown. One can be an artist or musician without the unction of the Holy Spirit operating in his or her life. These examples are talents, but the spiritual gifts are something totally different.

Charismata (spiritual gifts) are a manifestation of the Spirit and graciously given by God (1 Cor. 12:7). Talents can be learned and improved upon by human effort through training and/or education. However, the spiritual gifts are not earned; rather, they must be given to the believer by God and imparted by an anointed leader in the church (2 Tim. 1:6–7).

> Wherefore I put thee in remembrance that thou stir up the gift of God, which is in thee by the putting on of my hands (2 Tim. 1:6 KJV).

Paul expresses his deep affection in the letter to the Roman church on how he longed to see them coupled with his desire to impart some spiritual gift in which they would be established (Rom. 1:11). It is important to note the two things no one can ever take away from you: (1) your salvation and (2) your education or vocation. Your salvation is of priority in the exercise of vocational life and your life in the spirit.

---

[29] "Spiritual Gifts." *Nelson's Illustrated Bible Dictionary*, Ronald F. Youngblood, ED. (Nashville: Thomas Nelson, 1986), p. 1085.

[30] John MacArtur, *The MacArthur New Testament Commentary 1 Corinthians* (Chicago: Moody, 1984), p. 290.

For I long to see you, that I may impart unto you some spiritual gift, to the end ye may be established (Rom. 1:11 KJV).

The believer must strengthen their knowledge of pneumatology or the doctrine of the Holy Spirit in order to understand spiritual gifts (see 2 Cor. 3:17). The church's teaching on the person and work of the Holy Spirit must be based on the Word of God (see 1 John 5:6–8).

This is he that came by water and blood, *even* Jesus Christ; not by water only, but by water and blood. And it is the Spirit that beareth witness, because the Spirit is truth. For there are three that bear record in heaven, the Father, the Word, and the Holy Ghost: and these three are one. And there are three that bear witness in earth, the Spirit, and the water, and the blood: and these three agree in one (1 John 5:6–8 KJV).

The Holy Spirit is the third person in the Godhead (See Acts 17:29; Rom. 1:20; and Col. 2:9). There are three Greek words translated as "godhead." The Greek word rendered as "godhead" in Acts 17: 29 is *theios* (*thay-os*). According to *Bibleworks* definitions, it is the "general name of deities or divinities used by the Greeks." In Romans 1:20, the Greek word is *theiotes* (*thay-o-tes*) meaning "deity or divine nature." In Colossians 2:9, the Greek word is *theotes* (*the-o-tēs*) meaning "the state of being god, deity, or godhead." All three Greek words point to a supernatural or divine being that we call God in our vernacular. The divine being is multidimensional and multifaceted. In other words, the divine is manifested in plural ways.

In the beginning **Elohim** (plural noun of *El*) created the heaven and the earth. And the earth was without form, and void; and darkness *was* upon the face of the deep. And the **Ruaḥ Elohim** moved upon the face of the waters. And **Elohim** said, Let there be light: and there was light (Gen. 1:1–3 KJV, *emphasis added*).

God or *Elohim* created the heavens and the earth and all that dwell therein. We call God Father because he is the progenitor of all creation. The Hebrew word *Elohim* is the plural noun of the Hebrew word *El*, which is translated "god." In the Hebrew Bible, Moses understood the deity as he was instructed by the *Kemites* that *Amen-Ra* or *Elohim* is the one God who manifests himself in plural ways. The *Kemites* (or Egyptians) called the manifestations on the one God *neteru* or gods. *Neteru* is the Egyptian plural noun of *neter* (*net-cher*) (*which is translated as god*) where we get our word *nature*. In African thought, nature is the manifestation of the divine. The *Kemites* use the Egyptian word *ka* to describe the metaphysical reality that we call spirit. It is the vital essence or life force of God. It was considered the spiritual body and feeds off the prayers of the living. The Holy Spirit is the tangible presence of God the Father and the Son and is still active in the body of Christ today. Max Turner expounds on the Spirit this way: "Indeed, if one were to ask Jewish readers of the Hebrew Bible, most would have been liable rather to explain the Spirit as God's own 'vitality' or 'life'"[31] It is the vehicle by which God makes himself known. It is the energy-matter which manifests God's presence, wisdom, power, and revelation. The Holy Spirit is the organ or channel of communication between *Yahweh* and mankind. The believer has to get to know the Holy Spirit and how he works to grasp a profound understanding of his or her spiritual gifts. Do you know the Godhead? Do you know the one God who has manifested himself in three distinct but inseparable personalities called the Father, the Son, and the Holy Spirit?

And Moses was learned in **all the wisdom of the Egyptians**, and was mighty in words and in deeds (Acts 7:22, KJV, emphasis added).

---

[31] Max Turner, *The Holy Spirit and Spiritual Gifts* (Peabody: Hendrickson, 1996), pp. 4–5.

God is Father and begetter of his creation. *Yehweh* is spirit, and he is a personality who is personal God (John 4:24). We know he is personal because he has a name which he wants to reveal to those who seek him. He creates, sustains, and preserves his creation which he brought forth by the power of his Spirit and the spoken Word (see Gen. 1:1–3). God the Son was prophesied some 4,100 years before the first advent (6–5 BCE) through the Egyptian myth of Osiris (Àusàr), Isis (Àuset), and Horus (Ḥeru) on the African continent. Dr. Christine Hayes in *Introduction to the Bible* defines "myth" as "a traditional story—often fanciful and imaginative—that relates events in historical times, usually in order to explain a custom, institution, natural phenomenon, religious rite, or belief."[32] Herodotus (484 BCE–425 BCE), the Greek father of history, describes the Egyptians or *Kemites* in the fifth century BCE this way: "The Egyptians did, however, say that they thought the original Colchians were men from Sesostris' army. My own idea on the subject was base first on the fact that they have black skins and woolly hair (not that that amounts for much, as other nations have the same...)" [33] The *Kemites* or *Ta-Merrians* called the Trinity Àusàr, Àuset, and Ḥeru. In the African myth, we have the story of the immaculate conception of Ḥeru from his virgin mother Àuset. The world was introduced to the doctrine of the Trinity, the virgin birth, and the resurrection for the first time in this African myth.

So the story of the first Trinity was actually told on the continent of *Akebu-lan*, known to us as Africa thousands of years before there was a Europe. As a matter of fact, the pope still worships the Black Madonna and Child. The color of Mary and Jesus did not change until the late fifth century and early sixteenth century by Michelangelo's painting of *The Last Supper* in 1498. In addition, God and Adam were depicted as white by Leonardo da Vinci's painting on the Sistine Chapel ceiling called *The Creation of Adam* in 1512. Getting back on point now, God the Son was later prophesied

---

[32] Christine Hayes, *Introduction to the Bible* (New Haven: Yale Univ, 2012), p. 34.
[33] Herodotus, *The Histories,* ed. by BettyRadice, trans. By Aubrey De Sélincourt (London: Penguin, 2003), p. 134.

through the prophets of the Hebrew Bible and was manifested in the flesh around 6–5 BCE and dwelled among us. He was crucified around 29–33 CE and rose from the dead according to the Hebrew Scriptures (see Luke 24:25–26, 44).

> Then he said unto them, O fools, and slow of heart to believe all that the prophets have spoken: Ought not Christ to have suffered these things, and to enter into his glory? And he said unto them, These *are* the words which I spake unto you, while I was yet with you, that all things must be fulfilled, which were written in the law of Moses (the *Torah*), and *in* the prophets (the *Navi'im*), and *in* the psalms (the *Ketuvim*), concerning me. (Luke 24:25–26, 44 KJV, emphasis added).

God the Holy Spirit, the *Promise* of the Father, now abides in every believer. The *Parakletos* does not just come upon his anointed as narrated in the Hebrew Bible—the *Torah* (Law), *Nevi'im* (Prophets), *and the Ketuvim* (the Writings). Before Jesus Christ (*Yeshua*) came and died, the Spirit would come upon the prophets, kings, and leaders but did not abide in them. *Yeshua* described the Holy Spirit as the *Spirit of Truth* and as the *Helper* (John 14:15–18).

> If ye love me, keep my commandments. And I will pray the Father, and he shall give you another Comforter, that he may abide with you for ever; *Even* the Spirit of truth; whom the world cannot receive, because it seeth him not, neither knoweth him: but ye know him; for he dwelleth with you, and shall be in you. I will not leave you comfortless: I will come to you (John 14:15–18 KJV).

The role of the *Promise* of the Father is to tell the indwelt believers what *Yeshua* is saying, lead them in all revealed truth, tell them what is to come, and to bring to remembrance what they would need to know to fulfill their mission in the world (John 16:13–15).

> Howbeit when he, the Spirit of truth, is come, he will guide you into all truth: for he shall not speak of himself; but whatsoever he shall hear, *that* shall he speak: and he will shew you things to come. He shall glorify me: for he shall receive of mine, and shall shew *it* unto you. All things that the Father hath are mine: therefore said I, that he shall take of mine, and shall shew *it* unto you (John 16:13 KJV).

The Holy Spirit is the tangible presence of the Creator revealing his power, wisdom, knowledge, and will. The Hebrews used the word *rûaḥ* (roo-akh), which is translated as wind or spirit. The Hebrew language is descriptive as it depicts God's Spirit as the wind. The ancient Hebrews and Canaanites used the word *rûaḥ* (roo-akh) to describe the Spirit of God because it gives a visual image of describing the power of God. The wind is invisible and very powerful just as the God of the Hebrews is depicted. *Elohim* is invisible, eternal, and all-powerful. He is present everywhere at all times. God is all-knowing for he knows our thoughts from a far off (Ps. 139:2).

> Thou knowest my downsitting and mine uprising, thou understandest my thought afar off (Ps. 139:2 KJV).

One cannot discover or uncover the source of the wind or with absoluteness determine where it comes from. God has no beginning or ending, nor can one discover his origin. The wind can be joyous and resonant; likewise, the Spirit of God brings joy and pleasantness. As God's activity in the world, the wind can be relentless in demonstrating its power. As the wind can move objects in the direction of its will, so can God move people, situations, and revelation to the bent of his will. The Holy Spirit is gentle like a gentle wind or cool breeze that provides comfort to the one that experiences it. Finally, the wind can be penetrating by passing through layers that normally act as a barrier. God's Spirit is penetrating like the wind into the very soul of man which bypasses layers, walls, and issues when man tries to hide from God. Let's see how Jesus described the Spirit:

> The wind bloweth where it listeth, and thou hearest the sound thereof, but canst not tell whence it cometh, and whither it goeth: so is every one that is born of the Spirit (John 3:8 KJV).

What Are the Spiritual Gifts?

> Now concerning spiritual *gifts*, brethren, I would not have you ignorant. Ye know that ye were Gentiles, carried away unto these dumb idols, even as ye were led. Wherefore I give you to understand, that no man speaking by the Spirit of God calleth Jesus accursed: and *that* no man can say that Jesus is the Lord, but by the Holy Ghost (1 Cor. 12:1–3 KJV).

Paul begins by stating, "Now concerning things of the spirit, brothers, I do not wish you to be ignorant." Paul is responding to the Corinthians' letter written to him reacting to his first epistle sent to them which was lost (1 Cor. 5:9; 7:1) regarding the correct understanding of spiritual gifts. He addresses their inquiry about spiritual gifts by explaining the spirit world or the supernatural. Paul does not use the Greek word for spiritual gifts—*charismata*—but *pneumatikos*, which is an adjective translated as spiritual *things* or supernatural. The Greek word can imply "pertaining to the nature of spirits" or "pertaining to or proceeding from the Holy Spirit." It can also connote things "imparted by the Holy Spirit." [34] *How well do you know the supernatural world?* How you answer this question will determine how much you really know about God and yourself.

Paul goes on to say, "You know [*oidatē*] that when you were Gentiles (or unbelievers) in the company of mute idols even as you were led—you were being carried away." As with the Corinthians, unbelievers are being led by the evil spirits because they have the wrong understanding of the spirit world. There are also many in the church today who are led by the unclean spirits. Many in the body of Christ do not have an understanding of the supernatural world and spiritual gifts. The Greek verb *oidatē* comes from *oida*, meaning to know or experience is in the perfect tense. This means that this is a past action that has come to completion but still has an effect in the present situation of the writer. Paul reminds Corinthians of their past experience before coming to Christ Jesus, which they were currently aware of at the time he wrote to them. They remember their former state before coming to Christ Jesus and how they were being strung along by false worship and seducing spirits. They have now experienced something different, real spirituality opposed to pseudo-spirituality. He wants to give them better knowledge of the real presence of the Spirit instead of following religion which has no power (i.e., in the company of mute or dumb idols). As a matter of fact, the first gift of the *pneumatikos* is the enabling that allows one to declare that Jesus is Lord. In Hebraic thought, it is the equivalent of saying, "*Yeshua* is *Yahweh*!" Paul teaches that this cannot be done except by the power of the Holy Spirit. The initial step to understanding spiritual gifts is declaring Jesus's lordship over your life!

In the *Dictionary of Paul and His Letters*, the author pens, "The gifts were given to be exercised as a privileged responsibility."[35] In vv. 4–11, Paul gives us a category of the nine spiritual gifts. Why nine? The number nine in biblical numerology is symbolic of spiritual finality. When counting to nine, you come to the end of a cycle

---

[34] "pneumatiko, j." *The Complete Word Study Dictonary New Testament*, Spiros Zodhiates, Ed. (Chattanooga: AMG, 1992), p. 1186

[35] "Spirituality," *Dictionary of Paul and His Letters*, Gerald F. Hawthorne, Ralph P. Martin, and Daniel G. Reid, ED. (Downers Grove: InterVarsity, 1993), p. 913.

of numbers, and it begins anew at the number ten. It is also symbolic of perfect movement of the spirit.[36] The number nine is composed of the number three multiplied by three. The number three again is symbolic of spiritual perfection, divine manifestation, or God's mighty acts. The nine spiritual gifts are perfect and work together in threes for the full demonstration of the Holy Spirit.

> Where *there is* no revelation (*or prophetic vision*), the people cast off restraint; But happy *is* he who keeps the law (Prov. 29:18 NKJ, *emphasis added*).

> For to one is given by the Spirit the word of wisdom; to another the word of knowledge by the same Spirit; To another faith by the same Spirit; to another the gifts of healing by the same Spirit; To another the working of miracles; to another prophecy; to another discerning of spirits; to another *divers* kinds of tongues; to another the interpretation of tongues: But all these worketh that one and the selfsame Spirit, dividing to every man severally as he will (1 Cor. 12:8–11 KJV).

In verse 8, Paul lists the gifts of divine revelation. The Hebrew word for *revelation* or *vision* is *chazon* (*cha-zown*) which is rendered as "*vision*, as seen in the ecstatic state, or *vision*, in the night, or *divine communication in a vision, oracle, prophecy*" (BDB, p. 302).

These three gifts of divine revelation are the following:

➢ a word of wisdom (*logos sophias*)
➢ a word of knowledge (*logos gnōseōs*)
➢ distinguishing between spirits (*diakriseis pneumátōn*)

---

[36] John J. Davis, *Biblical Numerology* (Grand Rapids: Baker Academic, 1968), p.123.

Joseph Fitzmyer states, "The phrase *logos sophias,* 'an utterance of wisdom,' would mean the power to communicate profound Christian truths to others, because Paul is not speaking merely of the internal gift, but the way it is manifested."[37] It is wisdom given to any believer which is supernaturally imparted by the Holy Spirit and works in conjunction with a word of knowledge. *The Expositor's Bible Commentary* postulates, "The second is the ability to communicate with knowledge by the Spirit. 'Knowledge' [gnosis] in the biblical sense is to be taken as the knowledge of God's way of salvation through the cross."[38] A word of knowledge is when the Spirit reveals a fact to the believer about someone or something in which they never had prior knowledge. Many confuse this gift with the gift of prophecy. The gift of distinguishing between spirits is the ability to discriminate between spirits from God, the human spirit, or evil spirits. This gift gives the believer the enablement to discern the motives behind people, ministries, and other activities.

The divine speech or oracle gifts are the following:

> ➤ prophecy
> ➤ kinds of tongues
> ➤ interpretation of tongues

The oracular or vocal expression gifts include prophecy, which is speaking under the divine auspices of the Holy Spirit and is a known tongue. Speaking in different kinds of tongues is speaking in *unknown* tongues. The interpretation of tongues is speaking in a known tongue, giving an interpretation and not a literal translation of the unknown tongues. Murray Harris pens, "The ability to speak in different kinds of tongues has been taken to mean speaking in ecstatic, humanly unintelligible utterances, possibly similar to the ecstatic speech exhibited in pagan Greek Dionysiac expressions."[39]

---

[37] Joseph A. Fitzmyer, *The Anchor Bible First Corinthians,* Vol. 32 (New Haven: Yale Univ, 2008), p. 466.

[38] W. Harold Mare, *The Expositor's Bible Commentary, Vol 10, Frank E. Gaebelein, Ed.* (Grand Rapids: Zondervan, 1976), p.262.

[39] IBID, p262.

There are some who would like to argue that *glossolalia* is speaking in a foreign tongue or *xenoglossolalia* based on Acts 2:6. We will examine this argument later. Frank Stagg in *Glossolalia* argues, "The third usage is most difficult, where *glossa* is used for strange or obscure speech or utterance, now commonly called *glossolalia*."[40] There is no concrete evidence to support that the phenomenon known as speaking in tongues is speaking supernaturally in known foreign languages in 1 Corinthians 12–14.

> And when the day of Pentecost was fully come, they were all with one accord in one place. 2 And suddenly there came a sound from heaven as of a rushing mighty wind, and it filled all the house where they were sitting. 3 And there appeared unto them cloven tongues like as of fire, and it sat upon each of them. 4 And they were all filled with the Holy Ghost, and began **to speak with other tongues**, as the Spirit gave them utterance (Acts 2:1–4 KJV, *emphasis added*).

When discussing *glossolalia* or speaking in tongues, many begin their exposition with *the Acts of the Apostles*. The *Acts of the Apostles* was written by Luke, the physician and travel companion of Paul the apostle as early as AD 61–62 and as late as AD 100–130. One must also ask what Luke's sources were when writing about *glossolalia*. The genre of the *Acts of the Apostles* is a historical narrative. Luke wrote in a chronological order, so he had a source. I believe Luke's source on *glossolalia* was Paul the apostle and 1 Corinthians, which was written before the *Acts of the Apostles*. And 1 Corinthians was written between late AD 56 and early AD 57. If we can agree on Luke's sources, we must begin with the epistle to the Corinthians when trying to understand the spiritual gift of speaking in different kinds of tongues.

---

[40] Frank Stagg, E. Glenn Hinson, and Wayne E. Oates, *Glossolalia* (Nashville: Abingdon, 1967), p. 23.

> How is it then, brethren? when ye come together,
> every one of you hath a psalm, hath a doctrine,
> hath a tongue, hath a revelation, hath an inter-
> pretation. Let all things be done unto edifying
> (1 Cor. 14:26 KJV).

In Acts 2:4, Luke writes that the Jewish believers began to speak with other tongues. Some argue that these tongues were other foreign languages as they were enabled by the Holy Spirit. However, if Paul and 1 Corinthians were Luke's source, then the tongues would have been unintelligible utterances, not foreign languages. Paul describes an orderly worship experience as have a psalm, a teaching, a *glōssa* (tongue), and an interpretation. It can be deduced that at Pentecost, the Holy Spirit was the impetus of the sign of speaking in tongues and gave the Jews who were present the enablement through the interpretation of tongues to understand what was being spoken.

> To another the working of miracles; to another
> prophecy; to another discerning of spirits; to
> another *divers* kinds of tongues; to another the
> interpretation of tongues (1 Cor. 12:10 KJV).

The power *(dunamis)* gifts are these:

➤ supernatural faith
➤ gifts of healings
➤ working of miracles or powers

The *dunamis* gift of faith is not simply trusting in Jesus Christ or placing confidence in him for your salvation. This type of faith is the kind one has when they are in a hard place with no way of escape, and they are absolutely dependent on God for everything. It is the kind of faithfulness that is not easily wavered in the face of adversity. You will need supernatural faith to fulfill you mission and live your destiny.

The gifts of healings have to do with divine healing. This form of *pneumatikos* is plural. It should be translated as "gifts of healings." The Greek word translated as healing is *iama* and occurs c. 10x in the LXX. Most of the occurrences speak of *Yahweh Elohim* bringing healing and a cure to his people. "It is characteristic of faith in Yahweh to recognize that he alone is the source of all healing."[41]

> Nevertheless they sneered at his messengers, and set at nought his words, and mocked his prophets, until the wrath of the Lord rose up against his people, till there was no remedy (2 Chron. 36:16 LXE)

In the verse above, it is narrated that because the people mocked his prophets and cast off his words through the prophets, the Lord's wrath rose up and there was no healing *(iama)*. The scripture is clear that the source of this healing is *Yahweh*. Divine healing is the remedy to heal all ills that one experiences on their journey to their destination.

> If the spirit of the ruler rise up against thee, leave not thy place; for soothing will put an end to great offences (Eccles. 10:4 LXE)

In the verse above, the preacher called *Qoheleth* states that healing *(iama)* cause great offenses to cease and desist. This form of *pneumatikos* is not just about physical healing but also emotional and spiritual healing. They are gifts supernaturally given by the Holy Spirit.

> The dead shall rise, and they that are in the tombs shall be raised, and they that are in the earth shall rejoice: for the dew from thee is heal-

---

[41] i;ama, Moisés Silva, ed., *New Testament Dictionary of the New Testament Theology and Exegesis*, Vol 2 (Grand Rapids: Zondervan, 2014), p. 496.

ing to them: but the land of the ungodly shall
perish (Isa. 26:19 LXE)

Isaiah the prophet makes a correlation between the resurrection
and healing which comes from the Lord.

> For I will bring about thy healing, I will heal thee
> of thy grievous wound, saith the Lord; for thou
> art called Dispersed: she is your prey, for no one
> seeks after her (Jer. 30:17 LXE)

> Behold, I bring upon her healing and cure, and
> I will show *myself* to them, and will heal her, and
> make both peace and security (Jer. 33:6 LXE)

Finally, there is the gift of the working of miracles, an act of
power which can only be worked by God. It is a gift endowment
from the Holy Spirit activated by faith.

In conclusion, spiritual gifts are important to your life strategy.
They are evidence that one is immersed in and identified with the
Holy Spirit. They can help answer some of the most important ques-
tions you encounter on your personal journey to fulfill your destiny.
Ignorance to the teaching of the Holy Spirit and understanding of
the spiritual gifts can leave you lifeless in the church and in the world.

ABOUT THE AUTHOR

Johnny Freemont III is the pastor of The Anointed Word Bible Fellowship of San Antonio, Texas, and an adjunct professor of theology at San Antonio Theological College. He has been in the ministry for nineteen years and teaches Biblical Hebrew, Introduction of the New Testament, and other theological courses. He grew up in San Antonio, Texas, and completed his bachelor of arts degree at Huston-Tillotson University. He received a master's of art of theological studies from Austin Graduate School of Theology and a doctorate of divinity from Guadalupe Baptist Theological Seminary in San Antonio, Texas. He has been teaching theological course for over eleven years.

CPSIA information can be obtained
at www.ICGtesting.com
Printed in the USA
LVHW041934150920
666053LV00006B/589